THE LITTLE BOOK OF SALSA

Remembering Steven Johnathon George Workman Czeiszperger

George Martin Czeiszperger

Czeiszperger Publishing

Dedicated to
Steven Johnathon George Workman Czeiszperger,
Beloved Son.
1996-2014

INTRODUCTION

I sat with my shipmates at a tiny bench table in the ship's galley. It was a tidy little room with about 6 serving areas. The "Cranks," the name given to the men who serve time in the galley, would serve drinks, desserts, and take your empty plates. Well, except me, I could not eat the food. I thought to myself, "Another lie from my recruiter! This food is terrible!" Then I discovered Trappy's Louisiana Red Bull®! I was in Heaven! I could eat the slop that was an everyday occurrence in the galley. Just for the record, most Submarines have fantastic meals, it just so happened mine did not. We had the best budget in the fleet, but we did not eat well. Soon after, a case of Tabasco Sauce was discovered in the food stores. I graduated from Trappy's tang and zing to Tabasco's® Heat. I was addicted to the burn. After departing the Navy, I was glad to get a job offer at a Nuclear Power Plant in Wisconsin and I was off to a new adventure in Wisconsin. I brought my love of spicy food with me. I would grow pepper gardens every year and I would make 25 cases of salsa. This is what evolved.

PREFACE

A long time ago, when just a child, I often wondered what it would be like to be a millionaire. I asked my Mother what it might be like, she said, "You have to save your money for a very long time." I remember asking my sister "What is a million?" She took to pencil and paper and wrote the following: 1,000,000. She said, "It is one thousand- thousand." I wondered how one would amass such a number of one-dollar bills. Fast forward around 45 years, as I approach my retirement, I am constantly asking myself will I have enough to retire? Will I be comfortable in old age? Life has had its ups and downs and I am not halfway to saving my million. So, in a quest of boosting dollars for retirement, I turned to the internet and spent many hours researching the question "How to become a millionaire." I have read many self-help books regarding finances and wealth building. One suggested publishing books. I decided to become an author.

George Martin Czeiszperger, 06 June 2020,
The United Arab Emerates.

PROLOGUE

This is my first attempt at writing a book. It has been both fun and trying. I try to write about what happened in my life over a 12 year period when I was developing a salsa recipe while living in Kewaunnee, Wisconsin. The recipe took 12 years because I used fresh ingredients from my garden and you can only harvest a garden once a year. It should be noted, there was little overlap in my Son's life and the salsa recipe developmement. By the time my Son was born my salsa recipe had been mostly developed if not already perfected. I have placed my Son as a main charactor in this book to remember him and to allow his closest friends to salute and rememebr him.

CHAPTER I

*Just how many salsas
can you think of?*

What comes to mind when you think of salsa? Do you think of dancing with a beautiful Latina? Do you think of the many choices of highly processed so-called salsa found in your local grocery store? Do you think of gathering fresh ingredients such as onions, cilantro, lime, and peppers? What else might one add to salsa? Beans? Corn? Pineapple? The answer is just about any fruit or vegetable you could think of. Fruits are a nice touch and add a bit of sweetness. Various pepper species add different heat signatures. The heat signature of a pepper is often described in such words as slow burn, fast burn, climbing burn, short-lived burn, medium-lived burn, and long-lived burn. The natural chemicals in chilies that give a pepper its heat signature are known as Capsaicinoids. Nature provided six Capsaicinoids, industry has made a few man-made varieties. The unique blend or percentage of each Capsaicinoids in any particular pepper pod is what gives the chili its unique heat signature. Personally, I like a slow build and a nice after dinner glow. Would it amaze you to know that birds do not perceive the "heat" from a chili pod? Birds and peppers have evolved to have a great relationship in the jungles of South America. You see, birds do not have molar teeth for grinding food. In fact, birds swallow food whole, they do not chew their food. Birds that eat chili pods get high doses of vitamin A, which is good for healthy plumage shine. The chili plant is rewarded for not burning the bird that eats its fruit; the seeds pass through the bird unharmed and are then dropped with a small packet of fertilizer. The seed dispersion can be over several miles. Mammals on the other hand, chew or grind their food which would leave pepper seeds unfit for germination. But because of the Chile Burn that mammals can perceive, mammals choose not to eat chilis (except humans) So, one might conclude that nature has given the chili plants a defense against mammal. Most chili pepper species can be found in the Amazon Basin in South America.

Many species can be crossed for new and interesting offspring. Through a couple of generations of cross breeding, genes can be moved from one species to another through an intermediate species. There are 5 major species of

peppers: C. annuum, C. chinense, C. baccatum, C. frutescens, and C. pubescens. Annuum consists of bell peppers and jalapenos. Chinese consists of the habanero family. Baccatum has representatives such as ají amarillo, ají limón and criolla sella. The Tabascos belong to frutescens and the black hairy seeded varieties belong to pubescens. According to Wikipedia, there are upwards of 50,000 cultivators of the 5 major chili species. I, myself, have raised over 500 varieties. Getting back to the subtitle of this chapter, "Just how many Salsas can you think of?" The answer might be 50,000! In years past, in my desire to gain knowledge of both peppers and salsa, I have read many books and many pages on google. Salsa as we know it, is very much commercialized. It is filled with fillers and high fructose corn syrup. In less developed countries, Salsa recipes are simple and very much close to nature. In my research, I recall a quite simple salsa recipe.
The ingredients are listed below:

Chilies

Lime

Sea salt (optional)

I believe the recipe was taken from the Mexican Heritage; it has been so long since I read that literature that I cannot recall the source precisely. Two books that come to mind are "The Whole Chile Pepper Book" by Dave Dewitt and Nancy Gerlach or "Peppers: The Domesticated Capsicums" by Jean Andrews. I suppose if you lived close enough to the sea you would have access to salt, or you could acquire salt via the trade routes. The same would be true for the chiles and citrus. Prior to the Spaniards arrival, Mexico and South America had legendary trade routes. The point is it does not matter what ingredients are used in any salsa recipe; the earliest recipes consisted of the natural foods immediately available to the individual who could gather the ingredients. This too would make you think that there are endless combinations of ingredients that a person could combine for what we now call salsa. For the life of me I cannot recall the name of the condiment, common in Peru, that consists of thinly sliced red onions soaked in salt water for 10 minutes, a minced Rocoto pepper (C. pubescens), fresh squeezed citrus and salt. It is a fantastic meal complement. Soaking the red onions in salt water reduces the bite of the onion, a sweeter less harsh onion flavor is left. In the hills of Oxapampa, Peru, there grows citrus fruit that is green like lime on the outside but orange in the center similar to, but not quite like that of an orange. The taste of this citrus is likened to that of the limes we are accustomed to.

My Goddaughters in Peru will not be happy that I cannot remember the name of their cultural food! This dish has the basic ingredients of salsa, peppers, citrus and salt. Often, I travel to Oxapampa and barter with the local farmers for fresh peppers, they call them "Aji" where the 'J" makes a harsh "H" sound. I am all too happy to take over Rosa's outside pavilion kitchen located on the Native Reservation just a few kilometers from Oxapampa.

I treat Rosa to a fresh version of my salsa, she finds it interesting that I add carrots, celery, and radishes. Rosa has it "in the hand" so she can cook a meal without watching what her hands are doing and it will be one of the finest meals you have ever eaten! Sometimes I rent a room from her, sometimes I rent her tent and camp out on the lawn. Nonetheless, we have salsa with every meal, her version of salsa or my version of salsa. Maybe one day you can join

me at Rosa's humble pavilion. I mentioned celery, radishes, and carrots, and yes, I put these ingredients in my salsa. Occasionally I add sweet corn and black beans. I have made all fruit salsa with mangos, papaya, and cantaloupe. I have added shredded cabbage. I have added red beets. I have substituted leeks for onions. Perhaps a time or two I have used shallots. As you can see, you can modify any salsa recipe. All it takes is a little imagination.

You are making salsa to fit your taste, add what you like. Once upon a time, in the days when I had more time and energy than I do now, I raised all my tomatoes and peppers. I picked all my tomatoes and peppers. I washed said fruit and processed said fruit by hand. I even peeled my tomatoes after a boiling bath followed by a dip in an ice bath. What have I learned after all this hard work?

Well, now I buy stewed tomatoes in the can and use them as my salsa base, especially when I am going to place the salsa in mason jars and seal them for later use. I also buy peeled garlic; this frees up much time in the kitchen. You see, I use to peel my garlic a day before I boiled the tomatoes in preparation for peeling the tomatoes. I had two days of prep work before I even got to chopping my peppers. All this took place in the

small town of Kewaunee, WI. I would have friends over for a couple of days, peeling garlic, picking tomatoes, peeling tomatoes, and drinking beverages like we were still in the Navy. Making salsa in WI can be extremely hard on a person's liver! It would take two to three days to produce my 25 cases of pint jars.

 All good times but time is a commodity most do not have an excess of and as such you have to learn to work smarter, not harder. Quite frankly, nobody knew I switched to canned stewed tomatoes, nor did they care. If I am making salsa fresca, I will use vine ripened tomatoes vice stewed tomatoes. The last piece of wisdom I will share with you in this chapter is the use of vinyl gloves. Use them! You will not regret it. Many times, hours after I have chopped peppers, I have rubbed my eye, scratched my nose etc. and BAM those pepper Capsaicinoids set you on fire! The only cure is time. By the way, did you know Capsaicinoids are not an acid? Nope, they are a base. Did you know pepper seeds are not hot? Nope, the seeds grow on the placenta of the fruit pod, and the placenta has the glands that produce the Capsaicinoids. The seeds are "guilty by association" but the seeds are not hot.

CHAPTER II

Three Thirteen/Fifteen Thirteen

I was renting a small apartment in Kewaunee and living with the future Mother of my son at the time. Certainly, we felt the struggles of a young couple starting out with little to no financial education, training, or discipline. My neighbor was simply known as "Lucky Cooney". An ox of a man, he had shear strength, Cooney helped me clear land not too far off Church Road in the burb of Krok. I had built two houses on the 26 acres I owned in Krok. I bought them from a man named Charles, I cannot recall his last name, but he had spoken a life message to me when he sold me the land. He said "I have made a lot of money in real estate, and I cheated a few in doing so, and now I am dying and I will have to take those sins to the grave with me....whenever you deal with people, be honest and fair with them." Sometime around 02:45, Steven's Mother had contractions, we scurried down the stairs of our apartment and drove about a mile to the Kewaunee Hospital. Over the next half hour or so, the contractions became more frequent and powerful. It was not long before I saw my Son's head crown, I supported his head and waited for more of him to be exposed. When I saw his hands, I gently grabbed them with mine. His tiny hands wrapped around my index fingers and I pulled him into this world. Next, I cut the umbilical cord and officially named my son Steven Johnathon George Workman Czeiszperger.

The happiest moment of my life. I brought him into this world. The bliss did not last long. Steven's Mother refused to give up pot and I certainly drank my share of bourbon. Isn't it funny that, no matter how broke you are, you find money for substances?

To say I was broke-broke would not be fair, I saved the maximum amount in my 401K and I bought stocks as well. Still we lived payday to payday. I laid down the law, I said we were going to be responsible parents. his was soon followed by my credit card being stolen and my Son being taken to the State of Washington. Steven's Mother could not give up her drug abuse and refused to live in Kewaunee, Wisconsin. I waited 90 days and sent her a certified letter stating that she had 24 hours to sign custody papers or I would file charges, she would go to jail and I would get custody because I was the Dad and she would be in jail. She was facing around seven felonies along with credit card theft and falsifying her name at the airport. I flew to Seattle and picked up my Son.

I would raise him on my own for the next seventeen- and one-half years. Certainly, I would have let her have custody if I could trust her to do a good job, and I would have lived in a cardboard box to be able to afford a ticket to Seattle once a month. Truth be told, I could not trust her. As a result, I did what I needed to do to ensure my Son's well-being and safety. When Steven was three, I open-tuned one of my American Made Telecaster Guitars and told him to strum it. An open-tuned guitar is already tuned to a chord, so you do not have to try to make a chord with one hand and strum with the other.

All you need to concentrate on is strumming out a rhythm. Then I had a flash! I put a guitar slide on his tiny little hand and showed him how to plat slide guitar! I distinctly remember laying down on the couch one afternoon, seeking that deep and rejuvenating powernap.

I asked Steven to play slide guitar while I dozed into the twilight one. Even at three, Steven could play slide guitar. It was music to my ears and often I would powernap to his sounds. We did

all the Dad and Son things. We had pets. To name a few, we had Sally the salamander which we found almost frozen to death at Boy Scout camp. We had rabbits. We had dogs and cats. Briefly we had bluegill but that did not last long...they sure were tasty! Additionally, we played catch with baseballs, footballs, and Frisbees. We also had pedal bikes, quad runners, and a dirt bike. We built a "Man's Garage" dubbed the Garage-Mahal. It was 36' X 60'. It featured in floor heat, sky lights, a car lift, a paint booth, a weld shop, an attached studio apartment, an attached green house, and an attached lawn mower garage. But it would not be a Man's garage without a urinal rite smack in the center! Did I mention that the Garage-Mahal was home to three Mustangs?

Yes sir, we had a '66 Coup, a '67 Coup and a '68 fastback. And we lived payday to payday. Steven was active in the Boy Scouts; I became Scout Master of the troop we belonged to. It was a good time.

Steven made many friends. His friends spilled over to the 5th grade basketball team and wrestling. He kept many of these friends long after we moved on to Tennessee and Mississippi. Once in Tennessee, Steven joined the Army JROTC. He excelled at physical fitness. He could run for miles. He could do 100 pushups, he could out plank anybody! Within a year, we moved from Tennessee to Mississippi. Steven attended Southaven's Horn Lake High School. Immediately Steven joined the Marine Corp JROTC program.

His newfound friends were a tight knit group and did not immediately warm up to him. He got the usual hazing because he came from an Army JROTC program. Taking it one step too far, it was suggested that no Army JROTC Cadet was as strong or fast as a Marine JROTC Cadet. Steven suggested they run a mile and then do 100 pushups. So off they went running. Steven came in 4th place. His peers were giddy with happiness, they had beat the Army JROTC Cadet. But Steven did not stop running. He peeled off his 40-pound weight vest and ran another two miles and did 150 pushups! He told them he wore the weight vest "to level the playing field".

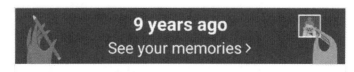

9 years ago
See your memories >

 George Czeiszperger
19 Aug 2011 · 👥

My boy switched schools and as such switched from Army JROTC to Marine Corp JROTC. The Mason lids were giving him crap about being an Army Dude....until they ran and PT'd. Steven took 4th in the two mile with a 40 Lbs vest on (nobody else had one) and he SMOKED them without the vest the second time they ran two miles, and oh yeah, they can't touch him in push ups or sit ups. He even beat ALL the cross country runners! What a dude.

From then on, it was Steven who was the anchor man for all physical fitness competitions. He was a machine. By the time Steven graduated from High School he attained the rank of Gunny Sargent.

He was the top-ranking enlisted cadet in the Horn Lake Marine Corp JROTC. Besides spending his spare time in the JROTC Cadet Program, Steven went to summer boot camps and he attended Boy's State. But he always played guitar. One of Steven's friends was Denver Massey, whom I am forever indebted to for his com-

passion and kindness in the years that followed. Denver was born with a half-length right arm.

He has a stub just below his elbow. Denver did not let this stop him from playing piano or playing guitar. He would often jam with Steven. Soon they formed a High School band. Steven asked me what he should say when the

potential band members asked him what he played. I said, "tell them you play guitar." Which Steven then replied, "I know Dad, what if they ask rhythm or lead?" So, I said "tell them you play guitar, rhythm, lead and slide, you are a guitar player, not a rhythm player, not a lead player, not a slide player, but a guitar player." Back to Denver and his band.

Many times, Denver has asked me for advice on managing a band. I share what I know. I give him financial advice, I give him sound gear advice, I set up his stage, sound, etc. Denver has many name versions of his band. To name a few that have been used are as follows: Denver Massey, The Denver Massey Band, Denver Massey Music, Massey Music, Chicken Wing,

and Broken Wing. See how I slid all those names in this book? My book will be copy righted and Denver will be protected when he makes it big, I will give him the rights to his band names. We were wondering how to get them copy righted. Problem solved.

In fact, yesterday, I proofread Denver's first recording contract. Look him up on Social Media. Denver was the first-person Steven visited when has was home on Christmas leave. Steven had left to become a Navy Corpsman. Here is what Denver has to stay about Steven, *"I first met Steven in high school my sophomore year. We were in home economics class and we had to write a song about food. At the time I was starting my band and when I saw him play guitar, I knew this could turn into something. He was the best guitarist I have ever met. Fast forward some and we are playing a few shows and we have grown close from practicing with each other all the time. We had a few fights and butted heads from time just like brothers, and to me that is exactly what we were, brothers. I have countless memories with him that I can remember vividly. From all the vehicles that we did stupid things with to all the guitar solos I heard him play to express exactly how he was feeling at that moment. We wrote a song together, he taught me more than I knew at the time about guitar, and we raised hell a lot. The last memory I have of him is when he came home for Christmas and I was the first stop he made. I was extremely sick at the time and I beat myself up about it all the time. I remember laying in my bed, next thing I know he ran up the stairs to my open door and yelled " WHAT'S UP!" I was so happy to see him. We went to the band room and we jammed out to "I Don't Want This Night to End" by Luke Bryan just like we use to. I miss him all the time and will never forget the joy he brought to my life. I love him as if we were blood and he will always have my respect."*

Denver Massey, June 2020.

I received a few letters from Steven when he was in bootcamp. All
and all, he was doing quite well. Immediately, he was chosen to
be the leader of his company. He was assigned Recruit Chief Petty
Officer (RCPO). In my day it was referred to R-POC (Recruit Petty
Officer Chief) and pronounced AR-POC. As in any group of people,
you will have conflict, bootcamp was no different for Steven. He
had one individual that challenged his authority when the Company Commanders left for the day. Steven used his skills he had
learned in his four years of JROTC and summer bootcamps. He re-
solved the issue, and all was good except one individual reported
Steven to the Company Commanders (CCs) who then relieved him
of his duties as Recruit Chief Petty Officer. The reason being was
that Steven should have reported the misconduct to his superiors
instead of handling it himself.

When asked why he didn't report the issue Steven simply stated
"You put me in charge, this is my Company, I handled it, we are
the best company on the street, look at our marks, SIR!" This was
too much for the Company Commanders to handle. They prom-

ised Steven he would regret coming to bootcamp and he would be going to IT (Intensive Training). This was supposed to scare Steven and when they asked him what he thought about that, Steven said "You're not my Dad, you don't scare me, you haven't lived with my Dad, you haven't been raised or trained like a Submariner, SIR!" And so off to IT Steven went. Upon arrival at IT, Steven was given a "MASH Card", it listed all the physical fitness exercises and repetitions that the Navy could impose on him. Steven finished the card without any trouble whatsoever and did not seem to be affected in the least, so they mashed him a second time. Most young men are crying or regretting they joined the Navy at this point, not Steven. (I remember my time at IT when I was in bootcamp, it was a ball buster!) So, they decided to MASH him a third time. Steven survived unphased, they could not break him. This continued for the next two days, still my Corpsman remain unbroken. On the fourth day, the drill instructor asked him "What he have you done this time, why are you back" Steven replied, "Same offense Sir, I maintained order and discipline in my Company SIR!".

The Drill Instructor replied, "I don't have time for this, I want to go home and eat dinner with my wife, you run until you break a sweat and then give me 100 pushups, besides I'm not going to break you." All this was not unnoticed, The Command Senior Chief (he was fulfilling the position of Command Master Chief) had been observing Steven for the last three weeks, he plucked Steven from his company and assigned him as his personal assistant. Steven was to write all the watch bills for all the recruit companies in Bootcamp. Steven was responsible for coordinating laundry and was introduced to budgeting and accounting. At the end of the workday, Steven was a "personal remote control" for the Senior Chief's TV. Steven would sit at attention, eyes forward, never looking directly at the TV. When the Senior Chief wanted his TV channel changed, Steven would change the TV, and then resume sitting at attention. The senior Chief asked him what

he would like to watch. Steven Replied "Recruits do not watch TV SIR! Recruits are in Boot camp to train to be Sailors, SIR!" So then, the Senior Chief asked Steven what he watched at home before joining the Navy. Steven Replied, "The Dukes of Hazzard and the Rolling Stones, SIR." And so, just like that, the Senior Chief was watching the Dukes of Hazard. On other occasions, Steven was ordered to "dispose of excess donuts" that the Senior Chief happened to have (fresh from the donut shop). Steven would "dispose of them" by taking the donuts to the trash, in the basement, next to the laundry machines. Steven worked for the Senior Chief from 04:00 to 22:00 each and every day. Often, Steven did not have time to properly make his bunk at 03:30, in the dark, while his shipmates slept. Then one day they had a barracks inspection, Steven's bunk took a hit. Steven knew he would be back at IT, but this did not scare him, not the least, and he wondered if somebody had altered his bunk while he was working for the Senior Chief.

Well now, the Senior Chief had the final say in the barracks inspection. He had everybody at attention and demanded to know why a bunk was left in the shape it was, especially on a day of inspection. Those that dare answer, stated "that's the way Recruit Workman left it, SIR." Then all hell broke loose, the Senior Chief explained in great detail what it means to be a Shipmate, a Teammate, and a Sailor. He explained that at sea and in battle

we have each other's back. The recruits in the immediate area of Steven's bunk got a turn at IT for not being a shipmate, for not being a sailor, and not having your shipmate's back. And if memory serves me correctly, the recruit who went to the CCs concerning Steven's handling of the issues a few weeks earlier, was now in charge of making Steven's bunk each and every day. Steven did not have to take time to make his bed and risk being late for morning muster with the Senior Chief. You see, the Senior Chief needed Steven in his office bright and early, coffee needed to be made, watch bills needed to be written, budgets needed to be reconciled and donuts needed to be disposed of. Soon after, the Senior Chief held a special on-the-spot uniform inspection of all companies in boot camp. The usual marching critiques were given as well as uniform discrepancies. Then something unexpected happened, Steven was called front and center and put at attention.

The Senior Chief took off one of his "Single Star Anchors" from his uniform collar and placed it on Steven's uniform collar. He then said to all boot camp companies standing at attention, "This is my Command Assistant. This is your ARE-POCALYPSE. He is the end all be all. Recruit Senior Chief Petty Officer Workman outranks all Recruits, he outranks Recruit Chief Petty officers. All Recruits including all Recruit Chief Petty officers will obey his commands. All

Drill Instructor and Company Commanders will execute all orders given from me through the ARE-POC-ALYPSE." About a week before graduation, Steven respectfully asked the Senior Chief to speak. Permission was granted, Steven said, "Sir, we graduate in a week, I have not marched with my company, I have not taken the physical fitness test, I have not taken the swimming test. I am worried I will not be able to graduate." The Senior Chief replied, "I have seen your uniforms, I have seen you bunk when you make it, I have seen your pushups, your running, your swimming, your marching, your command of the company when you marched them to chow, I have seen it all. You did not need to come to bootcamp, you were done before you got here. You were already a fleet sailor on the day you arrived, you just didn't know it." Later, I sent the Senior Chief a letter describing the events of December 31st, 2014, 03:15 hours. Many people have told me I was too hard on Steven, I was too strict. The Senior Chief thanked me for being the parent I was. He said, "Out of the tens of thousands of young adults I have put in the Navy, only Steven stood out to me as exceptional."

CHAPTER III

Moving the Sprinkler

T here I was, sitting on the sky-blue indoor-outdoor carpet that dressed my front porch stairs, there might have been 10 or 12 steps, but there I was sitting, playing guitar, drinking Budweiser, watching traffic. I had an Ovation acoustic; it was a prop for the band I formed and played in. Why would I say prop? Because a guitar-based classic rock bar band does not need no stink'n acoustic, all you need is an American Made Fender® Telecaster®. I had two, I did not need a stink'n acoustic, how lame is that? An acoustic in a classic rock band? Geeze, I must have gave into peer pressure. Do not get me wrong, acoustic guitars have their place but not in my classic rock band! As always, I digress, the story I am to share departed from my front porch to my thoughts on guitars: If continue to do that, we will never move the sprinkler...bear with me. My acoustic was tuned to open-E, which means the strings were tuned to an E-chord. I was playing around with some stand chord shapes on top of this Nashville type tuning, some may say it is a Mississippi Delta tuning. None-theless, Keith Richards uses open tuning and so would I. Did I mention, I have seen Keith Richards and the Rolling Stones four times and three of those times I had my Steven with me. As I was strumming away, I noticed that an E-7th chord shape played over an open E-tuned guitar gives a real great chord voicing! I was in love with this newfound trick. Later I would use this trick on my backup Telecaster on songs like Rambling Gambling Man (all due credit to Bob Seger, no plagiarism here). As I sat on my blue stairs, drinking beer, strumming my guitar, I noticed a peculiar man, standing off to my left, on the sidewalk, just before the sidewalk joined my walkway. I looked up and locked eyes with a man who had tennis shoes that were too wide and too long; the shoelaces were pulled tight so the opposite side of the shoe where the laces are strung were tightly bunched together. This caused the sneakers to wrap around his feet much like a corset you see in the old-fashioned cowboy westerns. His jeans were faded and over-sized as well. He had a thin worn T-shirt which was hidden under a second black leather jacket which sported chain that wrapped around one shoulder. This chain complimented a chain drive wallet that defied gravity: it refused to fall out of his back pocket that sported a hole in the bottom. The man wore John Lennon glasses, which were practical and not for show purposes. He sported long hair and a strawberry blonde "Joe Dirt" beard. In a humble voice he said, "Mind if I listen?" I shrugged my shoulders and kept playing. After some time and some strumming, Marcus managed to consume 6 of my 12 Budweisers. Soon he left for home. The next day, about the same time, who should come up the sidewalk with a 12-pack of Budweiser under his arm? As you may have guessed, it was Marcus. From that day forward we spent many days on the porch drinking Budweiser, Jim Beam, and other alcoholic beverages. Marcus was employed at the "Historic Karsten Inn." His duties included cleaning, dishwashing, rubbish disposal and snow removal. In fact, he did whatever he was told because he did not have a choice, he needed the job. One particular day, I invited Marcus to ride along to Green Bay with me. He gladly accepted and said he had not been to Green Bay for 10 years. Marcus was a castaway in Kewaunee, he had no money and no transportation, he was stuck in Kewaunee. I must have been Marcus's only friend, he spent a lot of time riding to Green Bay (we would get terrific burritos!), jamming guitar on my porch, jamming guitar in my living room, and being a roadie for my band. Marcus loved the Beatles, I loved the Stones, we both loved classic rock and alcohol. I was called into my boss's office at the nuclear power plant I worked at. I was asked several questions about Marcus. You see, people from work saw Marcus and I in Tisch Mills, outside a bar drinking beers and Marcus looked like an undesirable character, they had concerns of my character because I was seen with Marcus. I explained Marcus was my neighbor. I explained we often play guitar and go to Green Bay for burritos. My boss countered with "In this industry perception is everything, you have to be careful with who you hang around with, this Marcus is a left over Hippie that washes dishes for a living, you shouldn't be seen with him." I countered, "I wasn't brought up to look down on anybody." This is the same man who asked me not to get full custody of my Son because he did not need me distracted and he needed my full time at work. I did not listen to either of his suggestions, I still hung out and drank with Marcus and later I got full custody of my Son. I thought Mississippi would be racist and backward when I moved there, but there has been no place I have experienced that was more backward and racist than Kewaunee, Wisconsin. No doubt, Marcus was a lost soul in need of friendship and companionship. He was lonely. One day I came home from work and he said, "I hope you don't mind, I washed your dishes". On another day, "I did your laundry" and "I mowed your grass" etc. Marcus had become my housekeeper and lawn attendant. I reciprocated, as I have mentioned, by taking him to Green Bay and buying burritos. I would also drive him to Walmart and Kohls and other stores. Mostly we drove to the package store. He was my friend and I was indebted for his services. He really helped me out a lot. I friend of mine decided to go to Cozumel, Mexico. Robert had asked a few of us if me wanted to go along. The plane tickets were $199.00 round trip! How could I say no? I think Marcus felt a little left out when he heard of my trip, nonetheless he was happy for me. I could sense this in him. I managed to secure a ticket for Marcus. After all he had cleaned my house, done my laundry, cut my grass and shoveled snow for the last two years. I was somewhat indebted to him. The flight to Cozumel was terrible! Soon we found out why the ticket was only $199.00. The flight was tiny and over packed, the A/C did not work. We stopped along the way on several dirt road runways in the deserts and wastelands of Mexico. Every time we landed men in jeeps and armed with machine guns popped out of the sage brush and opened the cargo doors of the plane. Packages and cargo went in the plane and packages and cargo went out of the plane. Were we moving supplies for the Mexican Army or were we moving other things for other groups? Someone told Robert, "If we get out of here alive, I'm going to whoop your ass..." Robert, calm as always just replied, "We will be OK, I bought the tickets online, it's got to be legitimate." Robert was always cool and calm, and he was a great keyboard player. Occasionally he jammed in the various derivatives of the band I assembled. We did manage to arrive in Cozumel safely and Marcus was soon pickled in Mezcal in Cozumel. It was not long before Marcus and I were broke, the good news was that we were leaving the next day and our meals were included in our room. This was another point in my life where I had failed to see the necessity of having a budget and living within my means. My friends pulled me aside and expressed concern that I might not be having a good time because every evening at 6:00 PM I was taking Marcus back to the hotel and making sure he did not wander off in a drunken stupor. I told them I was having a good time and that it was my responsibility to watch after Marcus since I had invited him along. Truth be told, Marcus and I were both drunk by 6:00 PM and we were by all accounts broke as well. Then it was suggested to me that we make a rule that nobody can drink before noon on the next day, our last day in Mexico. They reasoned that maybe Marcus would not be intoxicated by 6:00 PM and may I could enjoy an evening on the town. I approached Marcus with this idea of staying sober until noon and enjoying the day and evening that would follow. Marcus was never one to debate or buck the system, so he agreed. We all met at the bar of the hotel at 11:45 in the morning. This was our morning muster and a chance to put out the plan of the day and agree where and when we would meet for a snack and later dinner. I was there with Marcus and all the other folks who were in our travel group. As we were ready to depart and see the sights on our last day, someone asked "Where is Markus?" A voice from the hallway said "Here I am! I made it till noon! I didn't drink till noon!" It was 12:04 and Marcus was shit-faced, he had slipped off and guzzled a bottle of Mezcal as soon as his watch chimed noon. The rest of the afternoon I did what I did best with Marcus, I watched after him and kept him out of trouble. Marcus and I did not go sightseeing, we sat at the bar and wasted away the day. We waited for the others to arrive for our final meal. By that time, Marcus had graduated from buzzed to noodle-man. As he walked around, he flopped and flayed like those huge air balloon figures that you see alongside the road at car dealerships when they have sales. Clark asked me "What's wrong with Marcus?" I replied, "That's just Marcus, he's having a good time." Clark said, "No something is wrong." I looked over in Marcus's direction and his jeans were soaked from his pockets to his knees. I took noodle man to his room. The next day at the airport proved to be a challenge as well. The flights were overbooked, and they insisted Marcus take the next flight. I was truly horrified, I could not imagine Marcus in a foreign country, not being able to speak the language and all by himself. So, I said to the lady at the counter, "Marcus cannot stay by himself, he has special needs, he cannot read and write and is very vulnerable." Marcus interrupted me and said, "I can read and write." To which I screamed "NO YOU CANNOT!" Marcus took the cue and repeated, "NO I CANNOT!" The Lady at the counter was on the fence, she could not decide what to do. Clark came forward and said, "I travel a lot, I will be ok, let this man take my place on this flight." I was relieved, Marcus was relieved, and we all made it home to the USA, except for Marcus. Marcus was detained by US customs and border patrol. He had the look and they were profiling. I politely told the officers, "He is with us, he is my housekeeper and gardener, I took him on vacation as a gift." After a few questions with all of us, they let Marcus come with us without any further problem. Never a dull moment with Marcus. One afternoon, after several drinks with Marcus, I asked if he was coming over tomorrow. He asked what we would do. I said, "I am watering the garden, I have 1500 pepper plants and they look a little dry." Marcus kindly declined, he mentioned he was not fond of gardening. I begged him several times, I ensured him we would have a good time. He kept declining; he was not interested in my pepper garden nor was he interested in maintaining it. He never came over when I worked in my garden. The next day, Marcus stopped by on his way home from work. He said, "I just stopped to say hi." I was on my garden swing, listening to WAPL, Wisconsin's Classic Rock Station. I handed Marcus a Budweiser, he accepted and sat down on the swing and talked about nothing for the next bit of time. I had three empty beers at my feet, Marcus had two, I pointed this out and said he was falling behind. He caught up. I moved the sprinkler. We repeated the process, we sat and talked, we listened to classic rock, we drank three beers, we moved the sprinkler. I explained to Marcus, every three beers we move the sprinkler. He said, "Ah, I like watering the garden!" The next day I came home from work, Marcus emerged from the back yard, Budweiser in hand he staggered towards me and said, "I moved the sprinkler four times!" Marcus had discovered the Joy of Gardening. Soon after, I never saw Marcus again. I heard he moved to Colorado, joined a church and was on a mission to find himself. Just as well, soon God would give me a Son to raise over the next eighteen years.

CHAPTER IV

John 15:13

D ana stopped over and helped me tile the shower on the first floor of my mother in-law addition I dubbed "The Granny Shack." Dana was exceptionally talented and learned quickly. She helped me hang siding, she helped me paint, she helped me hang drywall and if memory serves correct, she helped with a few shingles. Dana was my helper for the time being, Steven was in the Navy, he had graduated bootcamp and was attending Corpsman School in Houston, Texas. I had SRV playing in the boom box. Dana inquired about the legendary blues sounds she was hearing. I explained to her all that I knew about Stevie Ray Vaughn. Being as sharp as she is, she asked if that was why I called Steven, "Es-TeVaughn?" I replied "Yes, it is." I had few nicknames for Steven, this particular one was a cross between how his name is said in Spanish (Es-sta-ben) and Stevie (Ray) Vaughn. Dana was Steven's high school sweetheart. Soon, she was to be my daughter in-law. We would start our day just as Steven and I did, we would eat a bacon cheeseburger for breakfast at Huddle House, located in Senatobia, Mississippi. For lunch we would go to Taco Bell or Applebee's. At Applebee's, we would again have bacon cheeseburgers. Steven and I also frequented Hooters. We would always get Hot Wings; we had brought our love of hot wings from Wisconsin to Tennessee and then later to

Mississippi. In Tisch Mills Wisconsin, we would eat at John Lischka's Tavern. This Tavern was later to be sold to a man nicknamed Perv, the tavern was renamed Fatboyz. Steven grew up on Tabasco, hot wings, and my garden recipe salsa. He loved hot food. Being the character that he was, Steven often went to Buffalo Wild Wings with his friends and took the Hot Wing Challenge, he never lost. Steven would play guitar with the window open while I toiled in my pepper gardens. The same was true when I made salsa, he would play guitar and I would listen. One day in our apartment located on the edge of Southaven, and off Highway 51, Steven was researching the United States Marines. He told me he was going to be a Marine. I objected just as my Father objected when I said I was going to join the Marines. I spoke the same words to Steven that my Father Spoke to me, "If you are going into the Military, you are going in the Airforce or Navy and you will get an education." I served on Submarines in the Nuclear Navy. It was an education! My Father was right and so how could I be wrong by repeating my Father's words? Then Steven showed me a picture of a fallen soldier and a Corpsman attending him. The fallen soldier had a tattoo on his side, along the rib cage, where your arm would hang down. The Tattoo said, "Greater love has no one than this: to lay down one's life for one's friends." Steven said in an excited voice, "That's what I want to be!" I looked at the picture and asked, "You want to be dead?" Steven replied, "NO! I want to be a Corpsman!" In the months that followed, Steven worked out at the gym, did push-ups and sit-ups, and ran mile after mile.

He set up and staged battle fields with his friend Waylan where Waylan would play the injured soldier and Steven would carry him on his shoulder much like Forrest Gump carried Lt. Dan. Other friends would try to stop Steven from running with Waylan on his shoulder, they were the enemy and Steven would have to run through them and deliver Waylan to safety. Steven was obsessed with being a battlefield Corpsman.

Later I learned Steven chose Navy Corpsman for three reasons: First, I had been in the Navy; Second, he would get an education

and, lastly, he would still be with the Marines on the battlefield. Yes, he outsmarted me. Waylan was a goofy scrawny kid.

He was very naive and easily fooled. We made fun of him all the time, me, Steven, and the rest of Steven's gang. It was all in fun. Then Waylan joined the Army. One of the Gang made a joke about Waylan. Immediately I laid down the law! I said, "From This day forward, Waylan is a man. Waylan is defending our country, Waylan raised his right hand and left home, none of you did, you are not allowed to disrespect Waylan anymore." Waylan came home from the Army after his tour, no longer a naive child, he is full grown, full of self-confidence and can stand on his own two feet. The whole gang sees this in Waylan, and they respect him for his service. Waylan took care of me for a week when I needed help and I am forever in his debt. Here is what Waylan has to say about his friendships with Steven, *"I met Steven for the first time at school. He was two grades ahead of me, but we shared the same JROTC class. Some of the first things I noticed about Steven is that he was disciplined and head strong. He carried his self very well.*

41

He always excelled at everything he did, from being on the drill team or PT team with ROTC to playing instruments and everything in between. He always strived to be the best. We quickly became friends and he got me a job working with him setting up wedding venues for our ROTC instructors' company. From there we became even closer and we began to hangout quiet often outside of school. This is when I learned that Steven was an old soul and was born in the wrong time period. He only listened to 70s and 80s rock and would know every word to every song. Then I heard him play guitar and was astounded by what he was capable of playing at such a young age. Him and our friend Denver started playing all of the time. They even started a band. Unfortunately, I was never instrumentally capable so I would just hang out and listen and write some of the lines to the songs we would come up with. I always had a great time with them in the music room. Once summertime rolled around, we were pretty much always together. He told me his dad was building a house and asked me if I wanted to help. I told him that I did not mind at all. And we spent the summers putting siding on and building a two-story deck along the back side of the guest house. I learned a lot from Steven and his dad. More than they know. I miss Steven all the time and think of him every time I hear certain songs. He was stubborn and hardheaded as they come but he was more so a great person and had a good heart."

Waylan Moore, July 2020.

Daniel is another friend of Steven. Daniel and Steven connected on a different level. They talked about the medical field. Steven was to be a Corpsman and Daniel wanted to study medicine. Daniel would take Steven to Church. They were awfully close friends. As with all life plans, life happens, and we change and adapt our lives to what is put in front of us. Daniel became involved with the Fire Department and working as a build inspector and other jobs in  management positions. He was making good money and his life path has changed.

Daniel too has helped me out when I needed it. I am indebted to him as well. Daniels words of remembrance of Steven, *"Steven was a person that had a solid heart towards what's right. In every achievement he strived to be the best, while not only bringing himself up, but the ones around him. His attributes, skills, and personality where some of the best I have seen. He not only achieved his goals but had a passion to help others around him to help them achieve theirs. While life is a balance of many things to keep in the right direction, some many never figure out. However, Steven from a young age understood what was important. I truly believe he wanted to make the world a better place each and every day. They say the good die young and for me I can honestly agree. I miss my boy but know he with me every day."*

Daniel Hernandez, August 2020.

As Dana and I were installing tile in the granny shack, we made small talk. I mentioned that I hope Steven did not start smoking and I hope he does not start drinking. I explained he has an addictive type personality. He is all in in everything he does. She agreed with me, whatever he did, he did in extreme. Then I asked her if she heard a rumor that Steven had gotten a tattoo. She replied yes. I was furious. What the hell is wrong with him I asked her. She just giggled and said "I think it's a bible verse. It is on his ribs under his arm. "A Bible Verse! Why would he get a Bible Verse!" She said, "I don't know, it's something to do with John. He has another Tattoo; I can't remember what it is." I was steaming, I was hot! I could not wait for his next weekend call. I was going to give him an earful. He did call, I did not mention the Tattoos, I could not. He was now a man serving his country, I no longer had authority over him. Still I was mad. And what was this second tattoo? I guess I will never know...

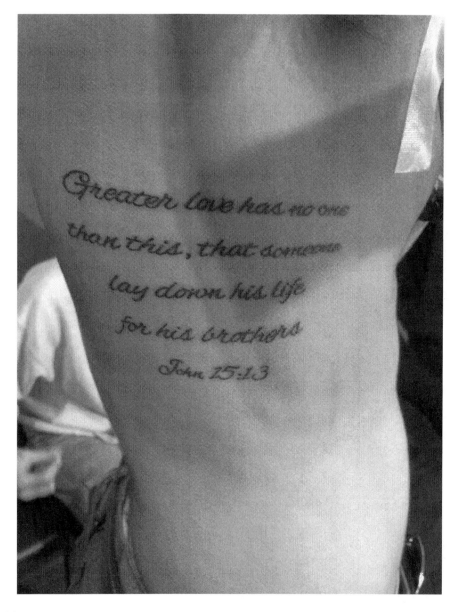

CHAPTER V

THEPEPPERKING

I had a couple of cassettes and CDs in my Ford Bronco II, Greatest Hits by the Cars and Stop Making Sense by the talking Heads, I am sure I had Toys in the Attic by Aerosmith as well as Permanent Vacation. I was tooling around the back roads of Oakley, Michigan close to my Parent's home. I happened upon Russ, who was a dairy farmer, he was bailing hay. I had been back in Michigan for a whole day. I was very much concerned about finding a job because it's embarrassing to be unemployed; even if it's one day, a man should have purpose and a job. I pulled over my Bronco and approached the tractor that was pulling a John Deere bailing machine, which itself was pulling a hay wagon. Russ looked at me long and hard, he did not say a word. The Fouss boys did not say much while working. Well, they never said much, but when they did it was worth saying and listening to. Looking up at the man on the tractor, I said, "Need some help?" The only reply I received was a hand gesture waving me up on the hay wagon. I had a job. I had pulled weeds, picked rocks, and bailed hay for Russ in middle school and high school. I was no stranger to hard work and long hours, however, in the last 6 years I had become soft because there was no labor-intensive work on my submarine, soon my hands ached from being worn tender and raw. The sweat oozed out of my body like the tunes that flowed from the AM Radio attached to the tractor wheel well fender. It was tuned to AM 1210, a classic rock station. Soon I experienced cramps in my ribs, I was depleted of salt and I was dehydrated. I could not believe the Navy had transformed me into all that I despise: a weak man that cannot do an honest day's work! I was embarrassed at myself. The sweating does have its advantages, it rids the body of toxins. I bailed hay for the next 5 days. I had a job. One week prior to my Naval departure, I attended a job fair in Norfolk, VA. I entered the civic center that hosted the event. There was less than 30 minutes left on the clock; the event would soon shutdown. I was in a panic; my future might be in this room but where in this room? After all, the clock is running out, there is a crowd and I have no idea where to begin. So, I made a large circle of all the company booths that were setup. I needed to see what was available, I needed to choose the most likely place I wanted to work. My heart dropped and sank without bottom, there was nothing that was suitable for me. Especially nuclear power. I despised nuclear power. I despised my recruiter and I despised the navy and its nuclear power program. I vowed I would never work nuclear again! I meant it. A small man approached me; he took the resume from my hand, he did not ask, he took it. He glanced at my resume and said, "Why did you get kicked off your submarine?" In shock (HOW DID HE KNOW THAT!), I said, "I made a tagout error, I made a mistake." He handed my resume back to me and said, "Be here tomorrow at 09:00. He pointed to a conference room. I walked away a little depressed, I did not find a job at the job fair, the clock ran out, the fair was done. I would have to return to Oakley, Michigan, unemployed and embarrassed; I could not find a job or make my way in this world. (HOW DID HE KNOW THAT...) The next morning, I arrived at the conference room. I sat at the far end of a long table, there were three interviewers who sat at different tables spread out among the room. It was awkward, one person would ask a question, the other two would be writing. Somehow, I knew enough to sit straight and move my head from interviewer to interviewer as well as make eye contact with all three. I gave short and concise answers, most of what I heard Chief Wickman,

"Wick-The-Dick", say during engineering department training. Q: Describe your duties. A: Training, Operation and Maintenance Q: How efficient is a Steam Cycle? A: Depends on Condenser Cooling Water Temperature. I can do the math that involves enthalpy, give me a set of conditions and I will calculate the value. Q: How do we increase pressure of the feedwater? A: Multiple stage centrifugal pumps. Q: We have a single stage feed pumps, how do we do we increase pressure. A: Your pumps must be screaming like a BANSHEE! Interviewer Comment: I do not have anything more; you are free to go. Internal thought: "You blew that one, you should not have tried to be funny and say, "screaming like a banshee." What is done is done, it is almost time to get to Zero's Pizza and make subs and pizza, and get drunk, again, at work, with the boss...." (I took a side job at a pizza joint to supplement my reduction in income, no more Sea-pay, Sub-pay, any other pay. I received a reduction in rank.) I was busted flat, and not even in Baton Rouge, I was waiting for my train, any train...Freedom is just another word for nothing left to lose...I felt I had lost everything, I lost my submarine qualifications and my nuclear credentials, I was about to exit the Navy and I didn't have a job. Being reassigned from the Naval Nuclear Power Program to a submarine tender was an eye-opening experience, I went from the cream of the crop, intelligent people, smart people, problem solving people to average people, and sometimes less than average. There was also a step change in everything, work ethic, morals, vocabulary, everything. The step change in working conditions in the Navy was nothing like I experienced at Zero's subs. Each day, at 16:00 hours, the ladies room turned into a pharmacy. Me being the hypocrite that I was, I protested their drug use as I handed them alcohol, all the while preaching to them about work ethics. I was so appalled at their morals and work ethic, their use of drugs, I could not see my own faults, I was drinking on the job. I could not handle these drug using civilians, I quit working at Zero's no less than 4 times. I needed the money, so like a slave to my debt and drinking, I went back to work each time they called. Would I ever be able to work with civilians when I left Norfolk in a week? I was home, I was at Mom and Dad's house. I had given my Dad all the money I brought home from the navy, less than $200 dollars. Six years in the navy and broke! My Dad refused to take the money but all I said was, "food and rent." My dad took the money, he must have known it would be an insult to give me charity. I was ashamed to come home broke. Sure, I had bailed hay for the last 5 days, but I knew not where I would be working tomorrow or the next day. I received a phone call from Kewaunee Nuclear, the lady on the phone asked if I had a credit card and if I was willing to fly to Green Bay for an interview. As luck would have it, I had just received my first credit cards. Sears, Kohls and a Visa. Later, I found out the credit card thing was a test, if you did not have a credit card, you would not get a job interview. I did not want to go to Kohls and buy interview clothes with their card, I did not have a job. So how would I pay my bill next month if I did not get the job? Eventually, I went to Kohls in Owosso, a 13-mile drive from Mom and Dad's house and bought clothes for my interview. I also purchased my plane ticket. I must have called a travel agent; these were the times before smart phones and certainly my parents would not have had the internet let alone a computer. The last thing I did before heading out to the airport was stop by Russ's house to collect my paycheck. I explained I was flying off to Green Bay for a job interview and I needed some money for food; in the back of my mind I wanted money for booze. He asked my hours and I report 20. He wrote me a check in the amount of $40.00. I said, "Thank you" and left. I was a little peeved, a little upset, a little hurt, a little disappointed! My ego asked the question, "How can he pay me $2/hr. like he did six years ago when I was a high school kid? Does not he understand that I just came home from defending my country! Doesn't he care that he cheated me?!" I was young and naive, I had an ego, I did not understand this is the way the world works, if you want more, you have to have to have an education, skills, and credentials. The plane started its descent into Green Bay, I looked out the window and saw green fields of hay. I saw tractors pulling hay bailers, pulling hay wagons. Just like the tractor, hay bailer and hay wagon I left at

Russ's house just two days earlier. The airport was surrounded by hay fields and I wondered just what am I getting into? The plane landed, I snatched a rental car and drove to Green Bay. Believe it or not, I did not know who the Green Bay Packers were, nor did I care. They did not play guitar nor were they the Stones. If memory serves correctly, I checked into the Holiday Inn, next to the Fox River, downtown Green Bay. I checked in and the receptionist informed me it was happy hour and that I should join the festivities. It was a Packer Party, one of hundreds I would attend over the next 18 years. After taking my suitcase to my room, I headed to the hotel bar. There was lots of food including brats and cheese curds. The food was free (more money for booze!). I sat at the bar and ordered a Beam and water. It came to $1.00. and two drinks were in front of me. Something must be wrong. One drink in Norfolk cost well over $5.00. The cost of booze was something I knew all too well. The bar tender informed me it was happy hour, which meant the bourbon was $0.50 or two for a dollar. Beer was two for $0.25. Suddenly, my $40 from Russ seemed like $200! At least in beer Dollars! Many of the local businessmen and women in the place were all too happy to spread cheer, when they learned I was on a job interview for the Nuclear Plant, they helped me celebrate by buying me several Beams. After my fill of free brats and cheese curds, I left the bar with $38 in my pocket, I was off to establishment number two. The morning I awoke and opened my clothes that I had purchased from Kohls. I hoped the "new creases" would fall out of the fabric before I arrived at the power plant for my interview. The drive would be about 45 minutes. I would leave Green Bay, due south, pass the Home depot and Walmart, hang a left (East) on Hwy 29 and drive 29 miles to Kewaunee. Once in Kewaunee, hang a right (South) on Hwy 41 and drive about 10 miles, maybe more. There she sat, Kewaunee Nuclear, on Beautiful Lake Michigan. I parked my car and soon I was in Miss Deb's office and was conducting a one on one interview, I believed she represented HR, I am not sure, I do not remember but it seems plausible. After pleasantries, Deb's first question was, "what did you do last night?" I felt my temperature rise, should I tell the truth, or should I fabricate a story, my future job was on the line... I cannot tell her I left the Holiday Inn and spent my last $38 on strippers. So, I replied "I played pool." She then replied. "Where at?" And I replied, "at the Holiday Inn, they had a buffet last night." She then paused, broke eye contact, and appeared to be looking at the various paperwork on her desk. She had trouble speaking, almost as if she did not want to but had to. She stated, "looks like your drug test came back negative." Again, I went into shear panic, it was just a week ago I had driven from Norfolk, stopped close to Pittsburg for the night and hung out with Mr. Stubbs, later to become Dr. Stubbs. My mind raced. What happened on that night in that little Burg next to Pittsburg? Stubbs greeted me with the usual manner. Big grin on his face, he said, "Hi Cheese!" Cheeseburger was a nickname I was given in the navy because that is what Czeiszperger looks like, so I have been told, again and again, ad nauseum. We went inside and sat down for dinner with his Mother and his Sister and had the usual small talk. Soon we were off to a quaint little bar where the bartender remembered us from our weekend trips from Norfolk, VA to Greensburg, PA. The bartender poured two glasses of milk, added tequila, and placed the concoctions in front of us. He remembered we traditionally drank "Ranchers, otherwise known as Colorado Mother-(F)uckers (CMFs)". Stubbs would always say, "Milk never had it so good!" Many times, over the years, this bartender would pay half, if not all, of our tab. He would thank us for our service. Soon we switched to old faithful, bourbon and water. This night we drove. On another occasions, we walked to this establishment. We would cut through an alley. The alley was home to a junk yard dog. A mean dog. Stubbs and I befriended the dog by sharing a pizza we had ordered and were eating on the way back to Stubbs' house. But that is a story for another time. Dr. Stubbs got out of the Navy on June 12th, 1990 at 10:00 am. One year later, I got out of the Navy on June 12th, 11:00. Exactly one year and one hour later. Steven was born on June 12th, 1991 and my God Daughter in Peru was born on June 12th, 2010. Enough with Calendar dates, back to my position with Dr. Stubbs in this book.

The Dr. and I left the bar and went to a hilltop offside the road. Stubbs told me stories of his camping trips, one of which he killed a wild turkey and roasted it over an open fire. The turkey was a bit small and scrawny, but he cooked it anyway. The Turkey tasted terrible, later, the Dr. learned he had killed a vulture and not a turkey. Dr. Stubbs, being a doctor and all, was a smart man. If he told me something, I believed it. He said vultures taste bad and as a result I have never had the desire to cook one! While we were up there, on the hill, exchanging sea stories and the like, I suddenly said, "HEY! Weren't we supposed to smoke a joint tonight? No more piss-tests for me! I'm out of the Navy!" We finished the last of the alcohol. I woke up on the couch. I quietly got in my truck and headed to my parents' house in Michigan. Honestly, I do not remember what happened the rest of that night. Only the good Dr. knows, he may never tell a soul, he would never betray me. Passing out was not new to me, it was just another night under the Doctor's care. I replied to Miss Deb, "That doesn't surprise me, I do not use drugs." And she countered with, "Do you go to concerts?" I replied, "Yes." Then she asked, "Is there a lot of smoke at concerts?" To which I replied, "Yes, the last Aerosmith concert I attended was so smokey I had to leave." Another white lie, the Aerosmith concert was two years earlier, it was the kickoff of their Permanent Vacation CD Tour, the night before we left for our 6-month Mediterranean Run. We left early because we had to grab our sea bags and be on the pier in a couple hours. Deb replied, OK I have a couple interviews for you with a couple of managers. Soon I was back in Michigan, my Mother picked me up at the Flint Bishop Airport. A week went by, there was no hay to bail, Russ finished while I was in Wisconsin, and I was broke. Later I learned, that when I was in Wisconsin, my Mother went to Kohls with my card and paid my bill in full. The rest of the week played out and I got a phone call from Miss Deb who said, "I'm not offering you a job"…my heart sunk, I blew it, I must have had a positive piss test. I had not sweated enough, the hard and physical labor I performed bailing hay was not enough to flush the toxins from my system, or was it? "But if I were to offer you a job, when could you start?" It was Friday, 7:15 PM, I replied "Monday." And she replied, "Don't you

need to pack, don't you need time off after the Navy?" Chance favors the prepared, I live by that mantra, as well as "shit or get off the pot". I replied, "I am packed, I own two T-shirts and a pair of jeans, they are still in my truck from when I drove home from Norfolk. I don't need time off; I need to work." Miss Deb replied, "Stop by my office at 07:00 Monday morning, I will start the paperwork for your security badge, congratulations." The next morning, my Mother took me to JC Penney's and bought me clothes and Red Wing work boots. I objected stating the boots were too expensive. But my Mother was in one of her 'command and control' mood, there is no changing her mind when she gets like that, and a stern voice and piercing eyes said, "NEVER MIND." If you know my Mother, "that was that" and you do not "poke the bear". My Dad calls her "the bear" for a reason. He has earned his free pass to Heaven! My Mother is tough. Off to Wisconsin I went. I used my Sears card to buy an inflatable mattress and a lawn chair for my apartment. I had a job. Each year, in Wisconsin, I would grow a pepper garden. It started out on a small scale, but eventually I was growing 1200 to 1500 pepper plants per year. I have grown well over 500 pepper varieties. Not all pepper species are suitable for Salsa. Some have too many seeds and not enough flesh, some have too much flesh and are watery when chopped and added to the mix, these types take extra cooking time to thicken up the salsa. Nonetheless, I was fascinated with peppers. I could not read enough about them. I could not taste test enough different hot sauces. I could not taste test enough salsa. I collected books on peppers. I printed articles from the web. I mail ordered seeds from every seed company I could think of. Still it was not enough! I had a flash, what if I could design a web site in which I could get free pepper seeds? What if I could get people to mail me their pepper seeds on their dime? Would people fall for that? How could I do it? What would make people participate? Are there people out there like me who are fascinated with peppers? Are there people out there who want new pepper varieties just like me? The answer to all these questions is yes, there are people willing to mail me their seeds, there are people who want new species of pepper seeds, there are people who want a central place to blog about growing peppers. I was using Netscape as a web browser; Netscape offered a free web design tool. Soon I created "THEPEPPERKING SEED EXCHANGE." Yes, THEPEPPERKING is one word. My webpage was simple to use. The directions were as follows: 1) Send me about 25 of any type of pepper seeds you have. 2) Give me a list of what type of pepper seeds you want. 3) Put a self-addressed, self-stamped envelope in your package. 4) I would fulfill your request or substitute any type of pepper seed I had in stock (there were no guarantees of what I had in stock). Soon my mailbox was overflowing with pepper seeds from around the world! Yes, I said around the World! I guess I did not figure on the World Wide Web making my webpage available round the world. But it did. I got packages from Russia, Japan, Sweden, Germany, Africa, Canada, Mexico, Italy, the UK and many more. I spent my free time opening packages and stuffing envelopes. It was a gas! We were at work, in the control room. We had ordered out, most likely Chinese. My friend John (Steven's Godfather) asked what I was going to do. We were out of Tabasco, Louisiana Hot Sauce and Salsa, the night shift had eaten my salsa left in the fridge. I reached in my pocket and pulled out a green chile I had grown in my garden. He smiled and said, *"The Pepper King."*

This is how I became,

"THEPEPPERKING"

CHAPTER VI

Something Sweet, Something Natural

I t was not unusual for members of the operating shift to bring in leftovers and share with the crew. After all, we were stuck on shift for 12 hours, either days or nights, and what else can bring a crew together like food? Ah yes, Power Plant Operators; whiners and diners! We did both! Perhaps, maybe I did more than my fair share of whining, but I hope to have passed that phase in my life. In Wisconsin, as anywhere, you learn to eat the snacks and treats the local folk partake in. Around the Lake Michigan shore that hugged Kewaunee County items of interest would include Krohn's Cheese curds and Knoop's hot sticks. I happened to live about 4 or 5 miles from either, it has been a long time, I cannot quite remember the exact distance. The other local staples include Miller beer and Kessler's whiskey, neither of which were allowed at work. Krohn's cheese factory was a local landmark and historical site, then it was sold to foreigners. A sad day for the locals who frequented Don's Outback Tavern, located in Krok, Wisconsin. Many a day, Steven and I would drive to Krohn's outlet store, located on the side of the factory. We would purchase several types of cheese, including 5, 6, 7, 8, 9, 10+ year old cheddar. The older cheddar gets, the sharper the flavor and the crumblier it becomes. We were privy to the private stash! But our favorite treat at Krohn's was fresh cheese curds, squeaky new cheese curds.

You might not know it, but fresh cheese curds squeak like basketball shoes on a wooden floor, really, it is true. Fresh cheese curds squeak when you chew them.

Back to sharing food on the night shift at work. We have mentioned cheese, cheese curds and hot sticks, but we should not forget natural hotdogs and bratwurst, both made by Konop's Meat market. But my favorite snack at work was salsa. One day Bob G. brought in a pint of homemade salsa for all of us to sample. I thought to myself, I got to make homemade salsa. I really did not know how to start. I did not have a recipe. I knew nothing about mason jars, preservatives, or canning techniques. Later I would learn that vinegar, salt, lemon, and lime juice are natural preservatives. I would learn canning from John Lischka. I was already in Wisconsin for a week. I had stayed at the Kewaunee Light House Inn, downtown Kewaunee. Work paid for the hotel stay, long enough to find a place to rent or buy. My week was up, and it was time to move into my luxury apartment right smack in the middle of downtown Tisch Mills, Wisconsin. Tisch Mills is a nice little town that had older people there when I arrived in 1991. All have passed by now and all have left a mark on my heart. George Prible was a wine maker. Mr. Klarek owned the general store and made homemade brats in the back. There was a bank and a post office. Just down the road was the Crazy 8 bar (fun times!). There was a ball diamond for the youth, a fire department, a sandwich theatre (served snacks while you watch a play) and Lischka's Tavern. The house I rented was next to George Prible's, which was next to the bank, the general store was 75 feet across the road and Lischka's tavern was kitty corner, adjacent to both the bank and the general store. I walked over to the John's Tavern and ordered a bourbon and water. The heavyset old man stared at me for a moment and asked, "What's that?" I replied, "Bourbon with water." He replied, "We doesn't have that, here have this." And he gave me a Kessler's and coke. After four or five drinks, I decided to head back to the house. I pulled out my credit card and put it on the counter. John poured me another drink and asked, "What's that?" Befuddled, I said with surprise, "A credit card." John then asked, "What's it for?" Still more confused, I said "To pay for my drinks." John just stared at me and said, "How do you do that?". So, I said, "You run it through your credit card machine." And John said, "Oh, I don't have a credit card machine." What to do? I was broke. I was living on my credit card till payday. I explained to John I did not have any money. He said come back tomorrow. I figured he wanted me to pay the next day. I borrowed money from the guys at work. The next evening, I went to pay my tab, but John refused to take the cash citing, "Keep it for food." He got me drunk again and said come back tomorrow. This went on for two weeks. I thought my tab would be a world record. He never did let me pay my tab. Not in the two years I lived in Tisch Mills and not in the 16 years I knew John. No good deed goes unpunished, I would get sauced up at John's Tavern in the afternoon and then go to the Crazy Eight until 02:00 AM. Then the phone would ring at 06:00, it was Sunday, it was John and we were going to church. I would sit there in church praying I would never drink again! John took me out for Sunday brunch every weekend and during the week he insisted I eat at his tavern, again, I never paid a dime. One day John decided we should go to the farmers market to get cabbage and cucumbers. We drove somewhere close to Manitowoc. I am sure we bought more than cabbage and cucumbers; perhaps carrots, cauliflower, onions, fresh herbs. After all, Lischka's Tavern had a full kitchen in which his sisters cooked every weekend.

A long story short, John taught me how to make sauerkraut, dill pickles, refrigerator pickles, garlic pickles, bread, and butter pickles. But let us not forget, he taught me how to can tomatoes.

If you know how to can tomatoes, you can make salsa. I could write a book on my times with John, maybe I will. Maybe I will name it Lischka's Tavern. John was an old man, never married, never had children. He was lonely I suppose. But I needed a break, I knew I was drinking more and more, and John gave me free alcohol night after night. So, I decided to leave Tisch Mills and move to the town of Kewaunee, in the county of Kewaunee. The last time I saw John was in a rest home. There was a chain across his door. The sign on the chain said "DNR." I entered his room; he was in a coma. I said, "John, you hear this? And I cracked a beer next to his ear." I sat in a chair, in the corner and talked and talked and talked. I told John everything I could think of. As I finished my 6th beer, I touched John's hand and said, "Goodbye Friend." Soon after, I went to his funeral. Another friend of mine who I spent many a time with would be Allan. Al invited me to join AMVETS post 99 located in Manitowoc, Wisconsin. I participated in a few go-kart derbies and poppy flower sales, but I was not interested in AMVETS. I was more into my guitar, various bands, Lischka's Tavern, the Crazy Eight, Outback Tavern and making salsa. Al was sort of a big brother. I would call him to help me look at houses I wanted to purchase, he knew the ropes and I was a 24-year-old greenhorn. Al and I would go to his farm not too far from the taverns in Tisch Mills and shoot our pistols. I got surprisingly good at hitting an empty beer can at 25 yards. We had plenty of empty beer cans and so we had plenty of targets. Al gave me both chives and rhubarb that grew on his farm. The cuttings were from plants that were over 100 years old. Eventually my chive patch was about a 1/10 of an acre, the same went for my thyme patch, it was also 1/10 of an acre. Both smelled yummy as I cut my 5 acres of lawn. The rhubarb cuttings grew into 72 rhubarb plants. I was very much into edible landscape, I guess I still am. I am sure Al influenced me when it came to home processing. I know we made sauerkraut, boned venison, and exchanged different pickles. Al was the only match for me when it came to eating hot food. In fact, we would bring in fresh cayenne peppers and eat them with nothing but fresh carrots and salt; we sprinkled the salt, bit a carrot, bit a cayenne, chewed, and repeated the process. I am sure we did this with habaneros and the other 500 species of peppers I have grown but I definitely remember the cayenne peppers. Al would also bring home made salsa to work, I would sample Al's salsa just as I would sample Bob G's salsa. I was hooked and wondered about the salsa making process.

I was obsessed with making a better tasting salsa. From the pepper patch I had behind my house in Kewaunee, recall the garden where Marcus faithfully moved the sprinkler, I handpicked peppers and made salsa in my kitchen.

My good friend Lisa, AKA Sister Kitty, often came over to help make salsa. Lisa and I would run it tight as often as we could, she liked her weed and I like my Beam. We formed a band; she played bass guitar and sang. Eventually, after 6 months of jamming in her basement and my front room, we scored Bob and Terry. Bob played guitar and bass. Terry played drums. Bob and Terry might have had an occasional beer, no worries, Lisa, and I made up for what they did not drink! We played a small circuit and had a following. The Band name was "Sister Kitty." Terry was a great drummer, and a good guy. Bob is a phenomenal guitar player with a pitch perfect ear. Bob could listen to a song and instinctively know the chord changes. Bob was accomplished on the guitar; I was a student. I learned from Bob, and we were a guitar team. I found ways to vary the rhythm by strumming full chords and playing arpeggios; playing single notes of said chord. A trick I learned from Eddie Van Halen. I also played as much lead guitar as I could. I had a Keith Richards feel on leads as well as "Southern Culture on the Skids." The latter, when they came out, sounded note for note like me. I knew what their guitar player was doing, I knew it came natural to him just as it did for me, at least this early rock n roll honky-tonk guitar style.

However, I was limited in my guitar vocabulary, I did not know all my chord inversions at this point and I barely knew scale pattern. There were songs I simply could not play rhythm or lead on (Ozzy Osborn's Crazy Train). Bob covered these songs and I fought with how to accent his guitar with embellishments with my guitar. Another song I could not get the lead down was Bad Finger's "No Matter What." Bob did the lead and then something amazing happened. Bob suggested I played as much lead as I could and then he would switch from rhythm to lead and I would switch from lead to rhythm. It was perfect! We did it seamlessly. Nobody knew we were changing guitar roles. This took the band to new heights, we were now a team, we were working together. I learned so much from being in Sister Kitty. I have imparted this knowledge to Denver Massey, but I still have more to work on with Denver, whenever I come home from the United Arab Emerates. Back to Lisa and making salsa. Lisa and I often cooked together, ate together, partied together, planted gardens, exchanged pickles, and made salsa, both individually and together. Let us get back on track. We started with operators at a nuclear power plant sharing food in the control room. As previously mentioned, I had sampled Bob G's Salsa and Al's Salsa. Both samples were acceptable, but for me something was missing. I did not know what it was at the time, but some of the best tasting foods balance sweet, sour, salty and spice. I stumbled upon it through years and years of salsa testing. My guess is that it took 8 to 12 years to perfect my salsa recipe. You might be asking why it took 8 to 12 years to perfect a salsa recipe. I might answer "It takes a lot of life to make anything worthwhile, a lot of life slips by while we do the things we love." Or I might say, "Anything worth doing takes sacrifice and time." In the case of my salsa, it was made with fresh grown tomatoes, onions and peppers. And, in Wisconsin, you only have one growing season per year. Therefore, it is reasonable to assume I only made salsa in the fall of the year when the garden presented and released its good to me. This was probably true in the early years when I used only home grown produce. I would bring my salsa to work and share with the crew. I would ask them to provide critiques. And they did. If the first feedback sessions were in my favor, well then, it would not have taken 8 to 12 years to have a decent recipe. I am sure my first batches were much like Al's and Bob's, basically a tomato base with onions and peppers. I am sure all three of us evolved our recipes at the same time; we all shared our canned goods.

It was just the neighborly thing to do, if we were going to be whine'n, we were going to be Dine'n! That is what operators do on night shift. With the feedback I received on my recipe, I eventually added garlic, lemon juice, lime juice, vinegar, salt. On my own accord I added cilantro, oregano, black pepper, carrots, radishes, celery, brown sugar and sometimes tequila or bourbon. You can see from my ingredients, my salsa grew and evolved into a "garden salsa" vice a traditional salsa recipe that one might encounter in Southern California, New Mexico, Arizona, or Texas. A good friend of mine, Mark, often gave me advice on a lot of things…and I needed it. Mark often taught me about gasoline engines. He was all excited and all too happy to help when I decided to buy parts for my 67 Fastback, my 68 Coupe and my 66 Coupe. Mark was a very technical motor head, he was actually on a pit crew, he knew motors. One day, while sampling my salsa, Mark said to me, "It needs something sweet, something natural." So off I went making batch after batch. I tried upping the brown sugar…no good. I tried switching to brown sugar…no good. I tried maple syrup… no good. Then one day, I dumped a quart of apple sauce into the batch. BINGO. The apple sauce worked. Nobody knew the apple sauce was added; the apple sauce quietly slipped into the salsa and could not be seen; it became part of the liquid. I kept it a secret for a long time.

And now you know THEPEPPERKING's secret ingredient for his salsa recipe. Other secrets and techniques used in my recipe include adding the following ingredients directly to pint jars before the salsa is added: Salt Brown Sugar Lime Juice Lemon Juice Vinegar Tequila (optional) Bourbon (optional) Rum (optional) The reason for adding these items directly to the pint jars is because they impart a different flavor when cooked. It was through trial and error that I figured this out. These ingredients imparted a better flavor to the salsa when they were not cooked. Once I knew the exact portions of each ingredient per pint jar, I thought

I could multiply the ingredients by the number of jars per batch of salsa and add them to the cooking pot. Did not work. The flavor was off. These ingredients need to be added directly to the pint jars with the cooked salsa. As I had mentioned, I have switched from fresh tomatoes to store bought canned tomatoes. Even spiced up or Italian style tomatoes work. I failed to mention that an alternative method to boiling and peeling tomatoes is to cut the tomatoes into quarters or eighths and liquefying them in a blender. The skins are cut too small to matter and curl up into hardly anything when the liquefied tomatoes are cooked down. I generally cook the tomatoes at a low boil until about 2" of liquid is boiled off. At this point I add the cilantro, carrots, radishes, celery, oregano, garlic powder, garlic, onions, chile powder, and peppers. Adding these ingredients cools the mixture to below boiling temperature. You must let the mixture return to a boil. You must constantly stir the pot, if you do not, the salsa will burn to the bottom of the pan. If memory serves correct, when you preserve produce in mason jars, the centerline temperture of the jar must reach 140 degrees Fahrenheit. Since my salsa had been at a low boil for a couple hours, as it boiled off 2", I reasoned the food borne pathogens would be eliminated. And I also reasoned, that when adding my remaining ingredients, the mixture needed to return to a temperture above 140 degrees Fahrenheit to make the salsa free of bacteria and pathogens. (It is the readers responsibility to follow FDA recommendations for home canning safety.) Last notes on salsa bacteria and pathogen safety; salt and vinegar are preservatives. Vinegar, Lemon, and lime juice lower the PH, which means it makes the salsa more acidic. The bonus here is that these ingredients also add to the flavor profile. Recall, we need to balance sweet (brown sugar), salty (salt), sour (Vinegar, lemon, and lime juice) and Spice (peppers).

CHAPTER VII

Eight Angles

S teven was home from the Navy, it was Christmas. Just as I had done when I came home on leave, Steven visited everybody he knew, except me. The apple falls next to the tree. I did manage to see him a time or two but as pointed out, he was seeing his Buds and his Gals…lots of Gals. He had rented a vehicle at the Memphis airport in order to drive from Memphis to the Naval base in Pensacola Florida. He was on a mission to pick up his MCJROTC friend, she needed a ride back to Memphis in order to spend the Holidays with her parents. I would not let him drive my truck, I knew that him and his friends would be partying like young friends do when they experience their newfound adult freedoms, just as I did when I was 18. Somehow or another, Steven ended up at our house for a brief moment the afternoon of December 30th. He was to fly back to Houston Texas and graduate from Navy Corpsman School. Daniel followed him in a separate truck. They stayed for a moment, made small talk in the driveway, and left. I did not even get to say goodbye. It was around 03:45 in the morning, the phone rang, I answered it and a voice said, "Mr. George, this is the Coroner." Fear swept over me, I interrupted and asked, "Is my Son deceased?" "Yes, yes he passed away about 30 minutes ago, a car accident." "Is anybody else hurt?" "No, single car accident, nobody else involved, you need to come down to the Police Station." "I'll be there as soon as I can..." I leaned my forehead against the wall. I said to God, "Just give me strength to get through this..." I remembered the story of Job in the Bible, Job had been inflicted with many trials and hardships, but Job never once lost his faith in God, Job always gave thanks. And so, I said to God, "Thank you for the honor of being Steven's Father here on Earth." I slid down the wall much like melted wax runs down the side of a candle stick. This wax isn't used, it isn't burned, it doesn't give off light or heat, it is just a mess of useless wax at the base of a candle; this is now how I felt as I laid on the floor. I could not get up, I could not clear my head, I was in a fog. I remembered a clip from a Brian Jones Documentary, Brian was the founder of the Rolling Stones. When Brian died, his manager said, "He is my boy, I protect him in both life and death..." Brian's Manager destroyed any and all evidence that would put a taint on the memory of Brian. He protected Brian; I did the same for my Steven in the days to come. First order of business was to squash all rumors that were already circulating or would be started; I made an announcement on Facebook. I would be the one who let out information. I called Daniel and said, "Steven's dead." Daniel agreed to meet me at the Police Station. Few other of his MCJROTC friends would join us. Later I found out they were not really friends; they were there to cover their butts. They had supplied the alcohol that Steven consumed that night. But let us not focus on the shortcomings of young adults, I am sure they have had to deal with this in their own way. I have forgiven them, but I never want to see them again. I arrived at the Southaven Police Station and waited in the Lobby.

It seemed like hours. Finally, a well composed Officer introduced himself as the officer in charge at the scene. He was the first person to care for Steven during his journey from Southaven, Mississippi, to his Final Resting place in Oakley, Michigan. He was the first person to care for me along this journey as well. He was a former Marine and he was the Police Department's Chaplin. A man of God; Angle Number One. He informed me that when he opened Steven's wallet and found his Navy ID, he immediately secured the accident scene to his presence alone. He would not let anybody else in, he recovered Steven's body, he made sure that Steven was handled with the utmost respect and care. We had some amount of talk at the conference table, I was still trying to protect my Son. I did not want him to be UA (Unauthorized Absence) from the Navy. I had one of his friends call the base and in-

form the quarter deck that Steven had been in a car accident and that he would not be returning. Additionally, I did not want the police report to say that there was a half case of beer at the accident scene. I said to the good Chaplin, the Officer in Charge, "I do not want a bad report given to the Navy, Steven is dead, he paid any price he had to pay." And so, it was. Steven had many friends; his friends would need closure. They would have to see him one last time. The following evening, Steven would be given a Military Funeral at Hernando Funeral Home, located in Hernando, Mississippi. The Chaplin who had recovered Steven's body would preside over the ceremony. The Horn Lake JROTC would be the color guard, and casket guards. In the meantime, I continued protecting my Son. I called all his credit card issuers as well as Navy Federal Credit Union. I told them the news and gave them a police report number. His accounts were frozen, nobody would be able to take advantage of his good name and use it for fraud. Additionally, I had to drive to the Millington Naval Airbase, located in Millington, Tennessee, and get a uniform for Steven to be buried in. Again, I was with his MCJROTC friends, one who was active duty, so we were able to get on base. I left the Police Station in Southaven and drove to the funeral home located in Hernando, Mississippi. Several of Steven's friends followed me. Inside the funeral parlor, I met with the gentleman who would process Steven. I asked if I could see Steven. I was allowed in the back of the building. As I entered the room, I saw Steven laid upon a table. He was on his back. A white sheet covered his body from his feet to his neck. He had cuts on his face, neck, and shoulders. His left cheek was discolored from a devolving bruise. He had both blood and clear inner ear gel leaking from his right ear. The back of his head as well as his upper neck was swollen from impact. The impact to back of his skull and neck is what dealt his fatal blow; he had rolled his vehicle and died instantly on impact. I placed my fingers on his eyelids. I tried to close his eyes, but they refused to shut. His eyes were perfect, beautiful brown eyes, normal pupils, normal whites. When I looked into his eyes, it was if he was looking back at me. I thought to myself, "What if I gave him mouth to mouth, what if I gave him compressions, I need to try.... did anybody try...I need to try..." Then reality set in, it was already 09:00 am, I was called at 03:30, too much time had passed, I could not save him. I tried to close his eyes again, they refused.

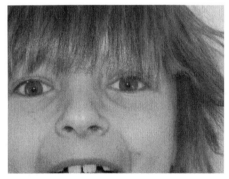

I kissed his forehead, caressed his face and rested my hands on his chest. I urged his friends to kiss him and touch him one last time. At first, they refused, they were horrified. I told his friends, you will never get to kiss him again, you will never get to touch him again, you will never see him again. One by one, they came forward and touched his face and said goodbye. I knew he had one tattoo, the Bible Verse John 3:15. I did not know he had a second tattoo. I was surprised to see when I pulled the sheet down to see the condition of his chest. I wanted to see how far glass from the windows had pelted his body.

I stopped pulling the sheet when a tattoo of a Buck Deer appeared on his right pectoral. I stopped at this point; I did not pull the sheet anymore. I did not want to see his other tattoo. I felt a strong need to respect his privacy, after all he did not want me to see his tattoos nor did he tell me about his tattoos. I had to re-

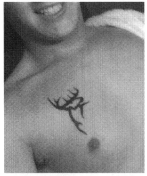

spect his privacy and his wishes. Sometime later Denver went and got the same deer tattoo on his arm in memory of Steven.

When steven's Sister Alex came to visit me, I asked her, "Why would Steven get a tattoo knowing I would whoop his ass, Man or not, Navy or not, I would whoop his ass!!!" Then I said, "I can kinda see the Bible Verse, it is a warrior thing, all the warriors, especially Medics get that tattoo, but why a stupid deer head, a waste of money, he always wasted money!" She looked at me and said, "It was for you, and it's a stag not a deer." I was a little shocked. "It had something to do with honoring you, he looked it up on the internet, maybe you should look it up." And so, I did, and then I cried. The meaning of a Stag tattoo is

many things and among them are Nobility, Royalty, Strength, Honor, Fertility, Renewal, Rightness, Masculinity and Virility. As much as we argued, he thought enough of me to get a tattoo to symbolize me. I am humbled. He loved Alex, later I found out they would talk on the phone every night without fail. Alex lived in the State of Washington and we lived in Wisconsin, Tennessee, and Mississippi. I raised Alex for about a year. Then after that, I only saw her once. Alex, her Sister (and Steven's sister) Nina and Steven's Mother visited us in Wisconsin. Steven was about 10. That was the first time he met his Mother and Sisters. It would be his last time. The next time Steven's biological family would see him would be at his second funeral in Chesaning, Michigan.

Alex stayed sober, but the others were high on pot and heroin. This is exactly why I chose to get full custody and raise Steven by

myself. For the record, I stayed sober as well, I had a Son to bury, I had a duty to perform, I stayed clean. It was the next day, December 31st, New Year's Eve. People had started to arrive at the funeral home as soon as it opened. Many would stay the entire day. I was busy folding American Flags with Dana. I was to present the Flags to Steven's MCJROTC friends as well as a couple other select friends. Dana did not know it, but she would receive a flag as I presented them later in the ceremony. I needed a break and so I went outside to walk the parking lot. Ben was in the Parking lot. Ben was a friend of the family; Ben's Mother was one of Steven's babysitters. Ben himself has had his share of hard times. Ben had an accident which left him bound to a wheelchair for life. Steven and I would see Ben at the gym, Ben was strengthening his upper body and I was teaching Steven to swim. Ben had seen my post on Facebook and drove all night to be with me at Funeral Home. Ben had driven from Kewaunee, Wisconsin to Hernando, Mississippi. That night Ben was my guest in the house Steven, and I were building. Ben was impressed with the doors, light switches, and showers; all were wheelchair friendly. I had been a member of an anonymous community for about two and a half years, it was something I decided to do to curb my consumption of spirits. Quickly I moved up the ranks and often chaired meetings.

I was introduced to "Pat in the Hat." Pat was schooled as a Preacher, he gave a great sermon geared towards the young people in the room, to comfort them, to keep their faith and hopefully to allow them peaceful closure. Pat was Angle Number Two, a man of God. Angle Number Three, another man of God, was John. John often talked at the meetings I attended, he knew every line in the handbook and he was very fluid with scriptures. He too, honored while talking gently to the young people.

ohn's choice of dress that day was a T-shirt that said, "Call to Duty." I believe the T-shirt was an advertisement for a video game that Steven often played. John's oration themed around the theme of the T-shirt. He tied both Steven's Duty in the Navy with Steven's call to a higher power in an effective and powerful manner. The Officer, Marine and Chaplin that talked to me at the Police Station gave the official ceremony sermon. It was a powerful message, I knew I was standing in the presence of greatness as he blessed Steven's MCJROTC Service, Steven's Naval Service, and Steven's Life. Next came Steven's friends, they played guitar and sang songs.

Denver Massey was the main guitar player and singer. Then, in an orderly fashion and with the help of the Horn Lake MCJROTC, and the Police Chaplin, I presented the American Flags. I had the recipients stand at attention, I said what I thought was appropriate to each, presented their flag and saluted them. The Chaplin and the MCJROTC escorted Steven to the back of the building where a hearse waited for him. He was to fly to Michigan. He would have a second funeral attended by his and my Family. He would be flown on Delta Airlines. The funeral director relayed to me that Steven may be stored in a freezer until the Navy could deal with the situation at hand. I would not stand for this; I was not going to let the natural processes decompose his body while we waited for the Navy to properly dispose of Steven's corpse. Steven needed to be placed in the ground, the sooner the better. Once again, as Steven's protector, I worked with the funeral director to have Steven's body flown to Michigan. He would be flown in the beautiful wooden casket his friends had picked out the day prior.

I let them choose because it would let them be a part of the process, and it would be part of their healing process. I did not know how I was going to get to Michigan. I was broke; I could not fly. So, I decided I would drive. I mentally prepared myself for the 13-hour trip, I had not slept in 48 hours, but I was going to drive. My phone rang... it was my lifelong friend Jack

(Bob) Brown. More on this call later in the chapter. Often, I would visit Ben while he stayed in Illinois, he was on a college basketball wheelchair team. Ben and I would hit it hard; we would drink like we were from Wisconsin. I would stop on my way through to Michigan, generally twice a year to visit my parents. On one such trip, Ben said, "You are blessed if you can count on one hand the number of people you can rely on at any time under any circumstance. I have five, how many do you have?" It was a scary question, what if I could not count five people that I could rely on no matter what? So, I held up my hand and counted out loud, (My Mother (one), My Dad (two), My Aunt Lauralie (three), My Son Steven (four), my friend Jack Brown (five). I answered the phone, it was a familiar voice, it was Jack. "Hey man, how's it going? I talked to the Legion, they bought you a plane ticket, you will have to rent a car at the airport." "I'll pay back the ticket." "Nope, it's on the Legion, it's taken care of, be at the Memphis Airport at 06:00 am, see you in Michigan."

And with that, Ben and I headed to my house in Coldwater, Mis-

sissippi. We both had to be up early, he was driving back to Wisconsin and I was flying to Michigan. I cannot remember the flight to Michigan, but I was to rendezvous with a Navy Detail at a hotel close to Flint, Michigan. The Navy Detail escorted me to the Detroit Airport. We were given access to the landing strip and we waited for Steven's flight to land. Two hundred Delta Air Line Employees assembled and stood in formation, a full color detail, complete with an American Flag, a Michigan Flag, a Navy Flag, and other Military Flags.

I was invited up front and presented a Delta Air Line Coin. The two hundred employees stood silent and at attention in that blistering cold night of January, they too were waiting for Steven's plane to land. Steven's plane finally landed. Delta brought forth a shiny new baggage conveyer/elevator, it was adorned with Army, Navy, Airforce,

Marine, Coast Guard emblems. One glance and I knew that conveyer/elevator had one specific use; it was reserved for America's Fallen Heroes. A young lad scurried up the conveyor with a battery-operated impact driver; he was to unsecure Steven's Casket from the plane cargo bay floor. He would not let anybody move the casket until he looked at each bolt twice as he circled the casket and then he counted the nuts twice. At this point, he said, "The Hero is ready to be moved, be careful, precious cargo." Then he exited the plane cavity. Next, the Navy Detail flanked either side of the conveyor/elevator, stood at attention and saluted. Meanwhile, the Captain of the aircraft announced to his passengers that they would wait for Steven to exit the plane before they would disembark. All the plane windows were full of faces watching Steven disembark via the conveyor/elevator.

Some windows in the plane had two faces looking out. Adjacent,

the airport windows were crowded with persons who observed the ceremony put on by both Delta Airlines and the United States Navy. Some could be seen crying for the Serviceman they did not know nor will ever meet. Others, presumably veterans, stood at attention and saluted and some people placed their right hand over their heart.

I couldn't leave Steven again, it was bad enough I did not fly with him and, due to my haste, he did not have a military escort on his flight, he had flown alone, by himself, unescorted.

It was my fault, I pushed the schedule, the Navy did not have time to get a Service Member to the Memphis Airport in time to join Steven. The best they could do was meet him in Detroit. I opened the passenger door of the hearse and got in. I said, "I am Steven's Father, I am riding with him to Chesaning." Off we went, in a driving snowstorm, but I was not scared, what did I have to lose? I had lost all that had mattered. I reasoned to myself, this man is almost seventy, he has driven in snow all his life. I felt at peace, I felt comforted.

I relayed my recollection of the Bible's Job, how he gave thanks, even in the worst of times and how I asked for strength to get me through all of this. The man talked about some Bible verses, I cannot remember the verses, but I needed to hear what that man was saying, it was what needed to be heard. The man finished with, "I am a Bible Verse Teacher, a Man of God." Angle Number Four. We drove to Chesaning and delivered Steven to the back door of Misiuk Funeral home. I drove home with Mom and sister Charlotte. I slept in the basement, my childhood room. The day, Steven would be shown at

Misiuk Funeral home. Many people attended. I tried to talk with all those I could, but I also tried to sit next to Steven as long as I could. I knew this would be our last visit.

My Mother introduced me to Chaplin Bernard Coonrod. Bernie, as he is known, was the American Legion's Chaplin. Bernie was about 85 years old, he was slightly bent over from a life of service, he moved elegantly, slowly, as he graced his American Legion Chaplin uniform. Bernie looked at me, we exchanged pleasantries. I said, "Steven has already had one funeral, in Mississippi, a Marine Corp Chaplin presided and prayed, but you may pray and bless Steven." Bernie entered a trance, his lips moved as he spoke some words, his eyes fixed on Steven, he proceeded to bless Steven. How I wished I could hear what Bernie was saying, but that was between the Chaplin and God. As Bernie placed his hand on Steven's forehead, he made the sign of the cross. At this moment, I swear to God I saw Steven's lip twitch; I said to myself, "He has been delivered." Angle Number Five, Bernie, a Man of God.

The next day both Steven and I arrived at the Catholic Church in Chesaning, Michigan, Our Lady of Perpetual Help. I was introduced to Mark, a Veteran, and a Chaplin. Mark belonged to a motorcycle chapter, comprised of Veterans. Mark's particular mission this morning was twofold; to honor Steven's service and protect the church service and grave side procession.

Mark had his biker troops flank the sidewalk that led into the

Catholic Church where Steven lay. The rank and file stood at parade rest, a military stance somewhere between "attention" and "at-ease." They were perfectly spaced. Their heads were forward and focused, they were disciplined Veterans. They were precise as they lined the sidewalk formation. Mark, or one of his Lieutenants, escorted my Parents (Steven's Grandparents), Steven's Mother, and other guests from the curbside or parking lot to the main entrance of the Church. One half of the rank and file were posted; the remainder of the troops stood guard at the graveyard, located in the countryside of the Oakley/Brady perimeter.

Mark Spent some time with me. He inquired about Steven's MCJROTC service and Steven's Naval Corpsman service. I handed Mark Steven's ribbons and medals he received from MCJROTC: Steven had many awards. Mark cupped the ribbons in both hands and held them as if they were the most precious processions in the world. Mark and I then placed Steven's awards in the casket. I stated, "I would like to keep these, but they are Steven's." Mark asked if he could pray for Steven. I agreed. Mark blessed and prayed for Steven. Mark explained to me his call to serve Veterans and his call to serve God. Angle Number Six. I entered the Church and tried to approach the Catholic priest with conversation. The man would not look at me. He was busy stroking a cloth he had draped over his arm. Three times I tried to strike up conversation. Still he would not engage in conversation, he was condescending and rude. My blood was about to boil, I thought to myself, "Who does this cock sucker think he is?" I looked up at the ceiling and realized I was in the house of God, and if anything, I would respect God's House. The priest acted like he was annoyed I was trying to talk to him, he asked in an annoyed voice, "How can I help you?" The thought that flashed in my mind was, "I'm am NOT in the mood for this shit! I am going to push Steven and his casket back outside and load him into the hearse." I pointed at the Casket and said in a stern voice "I am Steven's Father; I am trying to figure out what is going on here today..." at this, the priest fell off his high horse and tried to talk to me. It was too late; he spoke but I did not hear a word he said. All I knew was I did not want to be in "his" church, I did not want this man to perform a service for Steven and I wanted to leave with Steven. My Mother is an active member of this Church, she arranged the Funeral, she picked the songs and scriptures for Steven's ceremony. If my Mother were not so deeply involved, I would have pushed Steven out of the Church. The priest's behavior ruined my attitude for the remainder of the ceremony. I was glad the three previous Chaplains had prayed for Steven and I was glad they had blessed Steven.

Jack-Bob, had also talked with the local Police department and Fire Department. Steven would be escorted throughout the entire village of Chesaning. No detail was missed, all U.S. Flags were lowered to half-mast. The good people of Chesaning stood in the freezing rain; they waved handheld flags as Steven passed by. They stood in the freezing rain. Eventually, Steven would  leave Chesaning and head towards his final resting place.

The escort drove West, down M-57, towards the intersection of

M-52. Once again, I rode in the hearse. We passed the fire department as we drove down M-57. The sign out front of the Fire Station said, "Year to date deployments: 1". Steven was the first call of the year, I thought, "How fitting, Steven was always first in everything he did." It is a three-mile ride from Chesaning to the intersection of M-57 and M-52.

There was a freezing rain, and still, people stood at the ends of their driveways, hands over their heart and waving American Flags. There were people standing at the end of their drives for the entire drive from Chesaning to Oakley. People placed their 4th of July yard decorations on their lawns, on their house, on their mailboxes, it was amazing, the good people of Chesaning, Michigan. As we approached the grave site, a Fire Department ladder truck had its ladder at full mast, at the top of the ladder was an American Flag, riding the air currents in its full glory. Part of Mark's Veteran Biker Group was standing guard as we arrived; the Veteran Bikers who were present at the church arrived behind the hearse. The Navy supplied a detail to perform a Ceremony grave side. The Legion provided a color guard to perform Taps and to give a 21 Gun Salute. I performed an awards ceremony; I had folded American Flags which I gave to Steven's Sisters. I also gave Amanda a Flag. I met Amanda days before she left for the Army. After Bootcamp, she left for Afghanistan, she lost half a leg in battle. I presented her Flag and said, "Purple Heart, Wounded in Battle, American Hero." I saluted her. Steven's Great Uncles, Vietnam Veterans, were not present, they were in Texas. For each Uncle, I presented one of their children with a Flag, which would be later given to our Families' War Heroes. I could not watch Steven's casket lower beneath the ground. I remembered my brother's casket, I lost it when John's casket broke the ground barrier. I was not going to do that with Steven. So, I left. Maybe the next day, or the day after, I arrived at the Flint Bishop Airport, located in Flint Michigan. I would see Steven's half-sisters and Steven's Mother at the airport. I did not speak to them. I had only seen them once in 18 years, there was nothing to talk about. For a brief moment I lost track of what was going on; I saw a beautiful specimen of a lady. She was ebony in color, finely toned and sculpted as if she lived in a gym. Although it was freezing outside, she wore an athletic, half-length halter top. This allowed her abdomen muscles to proudly present themselves. I was thinking, "she must live in a gym." There was a delay at the gate but finally we boarded the plane and headed to Chicago O'Hare Airport, located in Chicago, Illinois. One, the planes were delayed in Chicago... The airport was filled with delayed people. There was no place to sit. There was no place to stand. Then I saw the ebony colored woman sitting by herself at a table in one of those airport restaurants. I asked if I could join her as there were no other seats available. We made small talk and she asked about the folded American Flag I was carrying. I explained how I had flown to Michigan to bury my son. I asked her what she was doing in Michigan, she explained to me she was in between jobs. She took a little vacation to see family before her next assignment. Naturally, I asked what she did for a living. She replied, "I work for Hospice, my specialty is to comfort family members who are about to lose loved ones." I would spend the next 6 or 8 hours with her as the planes slowly made their way back to the skies. She was aware of my grief and because of her training and experience, she was able to comfort me just by the presence of her company. Angle Number Seven. To this day, I still keep in touch with her on Instagram. Sometimes I flirt with her, sometimes she flirts back. But we always say hello at least once a year. I made my way to the newly assigned gate; I was stopped by two pilots. They did not say anything. They both stood at attention and with authority. One pointed at the folded flag I held in my hands. I said, "I buried my Son." I explained how Steven was home on leave and had a fatal car accident. I went on further saying that I had rushed things, that I had Steven on a plane before an Armed Forces Service Member could arrive to ride along and be Steven's escort from Mississippi to Michigan. By this time there were several pilots gathered around, maybe 10 or 12, maybe more. One pilot inquired as to the time Steven had flown. I responded as best I could; I did not know the exact time, but I knew it was late in the evening. One pilot spoke up and said, "Your Son was not alone, he was escorted, I was in the air at that time." And another agreed and several other pilots agreed and they too, spoke up saying, "I was in the air, he wasn't alone." One Pilot said, "We are all Veterans, we were in the sky, your Son was not alone." There was a moment of silence, I looked at these men, these Veterans, they looked at me. We shook hands and I left for my gate. Finally, I was on my last plane. Exhausted. I sat down. I buckled my seat belt. I pulled my ball cap over my eyes. I dozed off into the twilight zone within seconds. I was brought back to consciousness as I felt my right arm being bumped by the lady sitting next to me. She pointed at the American Flag that I held to my chest as I slept. I said, "I just buried my Son." Her words, her exact words, "You will be happy to know God sent me to be with you, I am a Chaplin." Angle Number Eight. As she spoke these words, I recalled all the Men and Women of God; The Chaplains, The Preacher, the Scripture Scholars, the Comforter, all who had been put in my path because I had prayed and asked God to give me strength.

CHAPTER VIII

PEPPERKING GARDEN SALSA

T o make PEPPERKING Garden Salsa, you will need the following ingredients:

1 Quart of Vinegar

1 to 2 Bottles of Lemon Juice

1 to 2 Bottles of Lime Juice

1 Bottle of Tequila (optional)

1 Bottle of Rum (optional)

1 Bag of Radishes 1 Bag of Baby Carrots (small bag)

1 Bag of Celery

1 Bag of Brown Sugar

1 Container of Table Salt (with or without Iodine)

1 to 2 Bundles of Cilantro

1 to 10 Cloves Garlic

6 Medium Onions

2 Red Beets (optional)

NOTE: Use as many or little chiles as you choose.

1/16 to 1/4 Cup Chopped Chiles (pick your favorite type or use a blend)

1 oz. Garlic Powder

1 oz. Onion Powder

1 oz. Oregano

1 oz. Chile Powder

NOTE: May substitute homemade Apple or Pear Sauce

1 Jar of Apple Sauce

20 to 30 Fresh Tomatoes (pealed or puréed)

OR

6 to 8 Cans of Stewed Tomatoes

24 Pint Jars with Lids and Rings

Step one in the process is prepare your glass jars for filling. The jars will have to be sterilized. I highly recommend that the reader research this extensively as failure to properly do this can lead to food poisoning. I suggest the reader use google.com with phrases like "sterilizing glass jars" or "sterilizing Ball jars" or "sterilizing Kerr jars" or "sterilizing Mason jars." I will tell you how I prepare my jars but in no way am I suggesting or telling you how to sterilize your jars. I may fill a 5-gallon bucket with bleached hot water and soak the jars for 10 minutes and then wash them in a dishwasher on high temp and heat dry. Or I may soak the jars in a kitchen sink with plenty of antibacterial dish soap and bleach. If I am using a dishwasher, I leave the jars in the dishwasher where they can stay hot until I fill them with salsa. Additionally, I sterilize my counter, table, cutting board, jar funnel, ladle, food processor and any other item or surface area that may come into contact with the ingredients during the preparation process. All the fresh ingredients are pureed in a food processor and placed in a large mixing bowl except ½ of the minced onions and ½ of the chopped cilantro. Half of these two items will be added to the tomatoes while they are cooking down. Preparing the pint jars. This portion of the recipe is manual; ingredients are added to the pint jars independent of the salsa mixture that will be cooked down. I have found that adding these ingredients directly to the pint jars greatly saves their flavor and enhances the overall flavor signature of salsa. For each empty pint jar, add the following ingredients:

NOTE: I use a total of three teaspoons citrus juice; 2 teaspoons lime juice and 1 teaspoon lemon juice. Sometimes I use only lime juice, and sometimes I only use lemon juice.

1 ½ teaspoon lime juice (see note above)

1 ½ teaspoon lemon juice (see note above)

1 teaspoon Salt

1 teaspoon Brown Sugar

1 teaspoon Vinegar

1 oz. Tequila (optional)

1 oz. Spiced Rum (optional)

The next step is to start cooking down the tomatoes. As I mentioned earlier, you can use fresh tomatoes, or you can use any stewed tomatoes that you buy at the grocery store. Using fresh tomatoes takes significantly more time. The two methods of fresh tomatoes are peeled or pureed. If you choose to peel your tomatoes, you will need to boil the whole tomatoes until the skins split and then plunge them in ice water and then, finally, you peel them. This method takes a lot of time. Personally, I have not done this method for the last 20 years. The pureed method is much simpler; cut the tomatoes in to quarters or eighths and then puree them in a food processor. The skins will be chopped up too small to notice. In either case, the next step is to cook down the tomatoes. The same is true for store bought canned tomatoes, they will need to be cooked down. Cooking down the tomatoes is easy enough, you simply evaporate an inch or two of liquid out of the tomatoes. I constantly stir the tomatoes as I slowly raise the heat. Stirring is necessary to keep the tomatoes from burning. Generally, I will have the electric stove burner set between 6 and 8. It is enough heat to bring the tomatoes to a slow boil without burning and sticking to the bottom of the pot. While the tomatoes are cooking down, I add the following ingredients: 1 oz. Garlic Powder 1 oz. Oregano Flakes 1 oz. Onion Powder 1 oz. Chili Powder 1 Bunch Cilantro, finely chopped ½ the onions, finely chopped Garlic Once the tomatoes have cooked down one to two inches, then the remainder of the ingredients can be added to the mixture. This would include the jar of apple sauce. Adding these ingredients will take the heat out of the bulk, but do not turn up the temperature on the stove. The heat will return in a few minutes, just keep stirring the bulk mixture. After the mixture is back to a slow boil, maintain the heat and keep stirring. Remember to intermittently turn down the burner as you scoop more and more salsa out of the pot. As the pot empties, the salsa will cook harder and faster and possibly burn to the bottom of the pot. I have my pint jars in the carboard tray packaging material they were in when I purchased them from the store. It makes it easy to carry 12-pint jars. As such, I place the case of jars, that are in the cardboard tray, next to the pot on the stove. I use a canning funnel and a ladle to fill the pint jars. I will scoop out the salsa from the pot and fill the pint jars via the canning funnel. I leave about 3/8" to 1/2 "of air space at the top of the jar. I quickly place a lid on top of the filled pint jar, with just slightly off center to create a crack so that escaping steam pushes out any air at the top of the jar. After about 15 to 20 seconds, I center the lid and place a threaded jar ring on the pint jar. The lid and the ring need only be snug and not over tightened. In about 30 to 45 minutes, the jars will begin to "pop" as the lids are vacuum sealed to the glass jar. Any jars that do not seal are allowed to cool to ambient temperature and then placed in the refrigerator for safer keeping. These jars are eaten first. The jars that seal can be kept on the counter for a couple weeks but, these two should be placed in the refrigerator. Once again, do proper research on home canning techniques from an approved source.

My method that I write about is for entertainment purposes only. I add my salsa to chile. I eat it with nacho style dipping chips. I put it on top of nachos. I give it away as gifts (I am always losing pint jars this way…) Enjoy.

PHOTOS

1

STEVEN J G WORKMAN
SN US NAVY
JUN 12 1996 ✝ DEC 30 2014
BELOVED SON

EPILOGUE

My travels have brought me to The United Arab Emirates, I am writing procedures for the countries soon to be commissioned nuclear power plant. I call it, "My Retirement Recovery Plan." While here, I hope to write several books. Two books will describe my adventures in the United States Navy. One book will be a compilation of the various sausages recipes I make in my studio apartment. Yes, I am making sausages in Abu Dhabi. I found a place to buy Boston Butts and smoked Spanish shoulders both of which I grind and blend with spices to make sausage meat. I hope to work in the UAE for 5 years. Lastly, I would like to start a YouTube cannel to help young people increase their knowledge of investing.

Thank you purchasing this book.

Respectfully,
George Martin Czeiszperger

ACKNOWLEDGEMENT

I would like to acknowledge all that have influenced my life and forged me into what I am today. No particular order. Steven Johnathon George Workman Czeiszperger, Corpsman, USN. Beloved Son. Steven and Helena Czeiszperger, Parents. The Eight Angles. Chief George Jackson, USN, USS Atlanta SSN-712. Chief Wickman, USN, USS Atlanta SSN-712. Master Chief Randy Allen, USN, USS Atlanta SSN-712. Master Chief Joseph Gallant, USN, USS Atlanta SSN-712. Jack (Bob) Brown, USN, USS Chandler EDDG-996, Sonar Tech. Dr. Stubbs (Hugh Hubble), USN, USS Atlanta SSN-712. Ray Guzzy, Track and Cross-Country Coach. Bob Segar, Track Coach. John Quader, Wrestling Coach Jay. Durham, Editor and Mentor. AA. University of Phoenix. Thomas Edison State University. United States Navy.

ABOUT THE AUTHOR

George Martin Czeiszperger

George Martin Czeiszperger THEPEPPERKING, A.K.A. Crazy legs, Cheese, Cheeseburger, Femmage and Stevie's Dad, was born in Saginaw, Michigan, 1966, at St. Luke's Hospital; delivered by Dr, Underhill. For the first 2 to 3 years, George and his Family lived in Saginaw Michigan on 2722 Ruckle Street but soon moved to Oakley, Michigan after Uncle Franky had a drive by  shooting incident. Uncle Franky was living with the family and was soon targeted by the Mexican Mob. George grew up in the country, he played baseball, football, and hockey. George worked for the local farmers picking rocks, pulling weeds, bailing hay, and milking cows. While growing up in the country, George often camped under the stars in the woods of Oakley Michigan. He fished in local gravel pits and under the river dam in Chesaning, Michigan. He perfected archery and trap shooting; he was an avid hunter and fisherman. George taught himself electronics by the time he graduated high school, he had a love for the electrical sciences. George taught himself to play guitar and played guitar late into the night. At aged 16, he joined the United States Navy and left for bootcamp by age 18. George's Navy evals evaluations stated, "Petty Officer Czeiszperger has established himself as a Hot-Runner in the Department" and was command advanced to Petty Officer Second Class. In the Navy George qualified Submarines, Nuclear Power Plant Welder, QA Inspector/Worker and Maintenance Coordinator. After the Navy, George became a licensed Nuclear Control Operator at Kewaunee Nuclear Power Plant. Over the next 27 years, George finished his degree and became a Nuclear Engineer. Additionally, George received a certificate of project management from the University of Phoenix and received two prestigious certifications from Project Management Institute (pmi.org), CAMP and PMP. George Is a qualified PPA procedure writer. Other Certificates include HAM Radio License and Distiller (Federal permit and State of Mississippi Permit). George loves classic rock and the Rolling Stones. His love for music often carried him through troubled waters; many times, he reverted to his guitar for comfort and escape. To this day his favorite bands are the Rolling Stones and Aerosmith. George's single greatest accomplishment was being a single parent and this was the love of his life.

CITATIONS

Andrews, Jean. *Peppers: The Domesticated Capsicums*, New Edition. New, Subsequent, University of Texas Press, 1995.

Dewitt, Dave, and Nancy Gerlach. *The Whole Chile Pep per Book.* 1st ed., Little, Brown, .

Made in the USA
Middletown, DE
12 October 2020

21759891R00064